SKINNER'S HORSE

SKINNER'S
HORSE

THE HISTORY OF
THE 1st DUKE OF YORK'S OWN LANCERS
(SKINNER'S HORSE)

NOW AMALGAMATED UNDER THE DESIGNATION

THE 1st DUKE OF YOR'S OWN SKINNERS
HORSE

COMPILED BY
MAJOR A. M. DANIELS, O.B.E.

The Naval & Military Press Ltd

Reproduced by kind permission of the Central Library,
Royal Military Academy, Sandhurst

Published by

The Naval & Military Press Ltd

Unit 10, Ridgewood Industrial Park,

Uckfield, East Sussex,

TN22 5QE England

Tel: +44 (0) 1825 749494

Fax: +44 (0) 1825 765701

www.naval–military-press.com

© The Naval & Military Press Ltd 2006

Printed and bound by Antony Rowe Ltd, Eastbourne

COMPILER'S NOTE

THIS brief history of Skinner's Horse has been put together in the spare minutes of a D.A.A.G., during the hot weather in Dera Ismail Khan. For its many imperfections it is hoped that readers will grant full indulgence.

This opportunity is taken of expressing thanks to the authors of the following books, from which much of the material has been taken :—Colonel Davies's " History of the 1st Skinner's Horse " ; Colonel Blakeney's " History of the 3rd Skinner's Horse " ; Fraser's " Life of Skinner " ; Cardew's " Native Bengal Army " ; Cavanagh's " The Reminiscences of an Indian Official " ; and to Lieutenant-Colonel Muirhead, who has written the last two chapters of " The 1st Skinner's Horse." Thanks are also due to Risaldar Shamshad Ali, late 3rd Skinner's Horse, and Risaldar Habibur Rahman Khan, Khan Sahib, Bahadur, C.I.E., 1st Skinner's Horse, for their very valuable assistance.

A. M. DANIELS,
Major.

DERA ISMAIL KHAN,
August 1923.

v

EXTRACTS FROM ARMY LISTS

FOREWORD

Eleven years ago " The History of the 3rd Skinner's Horse " was commenced by Major A. M. Daniels at the earnest request of all the Officers then present with the Regiment.

This history never got into print owing to the manuscript, as well as the old Digest of services of the Regiment, being stolen as Major (then Captain) A. M. Daniels was proceeding across Italy by train whilst going home on furlough.

The Great War then intervened and all hopes of re-starting the compilation had to be abandoned until the return of such pre-war officers as remained from the various fronts on which they had been engaged. There-fore, it remained undone until the reduction, conversion, and amalgamation scheme for the Indian Cavalry had issued.

Under this scheme the two Regiments bearing the famous name of Skinner's Horse, viz. 1st D.Y.O. Lancers (Skinner's Horse) and 3rd Skinner's Horse, were naturally selected to amalgamate, at first under the name of 1st/3rd Cavalry, and later under its present designation 1st D.Y.O. Skinner's Horse.

Having had the honour of being appointed Commandant of the present Regiment prior to its amalgamation and reconstruction, I approached Major A. M. Daniels with a view to restarting a combined history of the two Regiments on the lines of the previous one.

This he very kindly consented to do, despite the heavy duties he was called upon to perform as D.A.A.G. to the Wazirforce Staff.

I am sure that all officers of the Regiment, both past and present, will join with me in thanking Major A. M. Daniels for this history of one of the famous old Indian Cavalry Regiments.

E. C. W. CONWAY-GORDON,
Lieutenant-Colonel, Commandant
1st Duke of York's Own Skinner's Horse.

FEROZEPORE,
    4th May 1924.

SKINNER'S HORSE

1ST CORPS.—Raised in 1803 from a body of Perron's Horse in the service of the Maharajah Scindhia. Became the 1st Duke of York's Own Lancers (Skinner's Horse). Amalgamated with the 2nd Corps in 1921.

2ND CORPS.—Raised in 1814. Became the 3rd Skinner's Horse. Amalgamated with the 1st Corps in 1921.

3RD CORPS.—Raised in 1814. Disbanded in 1819.

Some explanation seems necessary of the various designations under which the 1st and 2nd Corps have been known.

When raised, the Corps was originally styled: " Captain Skinner's Corps of Irregular Horse," a designation soon abbreviated into " Skinner's Horse." On expansion in 1814 into three Corps these were designated: The 1st, 2nd, and 3rd Corps of " Lieutenant-Colonel Skinner's Irregular Horse."

When Captain Baddeley succeeded Robert Skinner in command of the 2nd Corps in 1821, this Corps was renamed " Baddeley's Frontier Horse."

In 1823 the five Corps of Irregular Horse in the Bengal Army were redesignated as Local Horse and given numbers according to seniority. The 1st Corps became " The 1st Regiment of Local Horse," and the 2nd Corps " The 4th Regiment of Local Horse." As these Corps were employed on foreign service, the designation " Local Horse " seemed inappropriate, and in 1840 was changed to " Irregular Cavalry," the two Corps becoming " The 1st Bengal Irregular Cavalry " and " The 4th Bengal Irregular Cavalry " respectively.

In 1861, on the reorganisation of the Bengal Army after the Mutiny, the designation of the two Corps became " The 1st Regiment of Bengal Cavalry " and " The 3rd Regiment of Bengal Cavalry."

In 1896 the 1st Corps became " The 1st Regiment of Bengal Lancers," and in 1899 " The 1st (Duke of York's Own) Regiment of Bengal Lancers."

In 1901 the two Corps became " The 1st (Duke of York's Own) Bengal Lancers (Skinner's Horse) " and " The 3rd Bengal Cavalry (Skinner's Horse) " respectively.

Consequent to the abolition of the Presidency Armies in 1895 and the formation of the Indian Army as announced at the Delhi Durbar of 1903, the designation of the two Corps in the latter year became " The 1st Duke of York's Own Lancers (Skinner's Horse) " and " The 3rd Skinner's Horse."

In 1921 these two Corps were amalgamated, and received in 1922 the designation " The 1st Duke of York's Own Skinner's Horse."

CONTENTS

PART I

CAPTAIN SKINNER'S CORPS OF IRREGULAR HORSE

CHAPTER I

1803–1814

CHAPTER II

1814–1819

PART II

THE 1ST CORPS OR 1ST DUKE OF YORK'S OWN LANCERS (SKINNER'S HORSE)

CHAPTER III

1819–1841

CONTENTS

PART III

THE 2ND CORPS OR THE 3RD SKINNER'S HORSE

CHAPTER XII
1842–1856

CHAPTER XIII
1857–1859

CHAPTER XIV
1860–1880

CHAPTER XV
1881–1899

CHAPTER XVI
1901–1914

CHAPTER XVII
1914–1921

CONTENTS

APPENDIX A

APPENDIX B

APPENDIX C

APPENDIX D

PART I

CAPTAIN SKINNER'S CORPS OF IRREGULAR HORSE

CHAPTER I

1803–1814

SKINNER'S HORSE takes us back to the days of Count de
Boigne and Perron, commanders of Scindhia's Regular
Army in the latter half of the eighteenth century. These
distinguished French soldiers had raised and organised an
army for Scindhia on European lines. In his army
Scindhia employed many European officers, but on his
declaration of war with the Honourable East India
Company, all Europeans of British descent were dismissed
from his service. Among these were James Skinner and
his brother Robert Skinner.

The year was 1803. Perron was in flight to Agra, and
the Mahratta mass which he had thrown in vain across the
victorious path of Lake had shattered into fragments
and fled, some towards Delhi and some towards their
homes. At Delhi, Bourquien attempted to oppose the
British General, and again the Mahrattas were defeated
with great slaughter. To fight and be defeated was an
experience new to Scindhia's battalions, and after that
terrible fight at Delhi, of which for many a day the Jumna
told a tale of fearful carnage, Mahratta troops came in
to lend their swords to the victors. And such was the
origin of " Skinner's Horse."

Delhi had fallen but a few days when the news was
brought to Lord Lake that eight risalahs, each of one

3

hundred horse, belonging to Perron's force, had arrived in camp to offer their services to the British. Right willingly was their offer taken. But those men would only fight for us on one condition, namely, that they should choose their leader for themselves and never be led against their old master Scindhia. They made their choice, " The Burra Sekunder," James Skinner.

Skinner's father was a Scotchman, his mother a Rajpootnee prisoner of war, who fell into the hands of Ensign Skinner, and became by him the mother of six children, afterwards committing suicide because her girls were taken from behind the purdah to become the wives of men in the Company's service. Of the boys, one became a sailor, and James and Robert soldiers. James was first apprenticed to a printer, but ran away after thirty-six hours of office experience, and lived for some time in the bazaars, on two annas a day, as assistant to native carpenters. A relative, however, found him out, and sent him to General de Boigne, commanding the Mahratta Army at Coel, who gave him a commission in Scindhia's service as ensign. Skinner soon became distinguished even among his sowars for his skill with the lance and sword, and after his marvellous gallantry at Chundkeree was promoted to lieutenant.

But this is not the place to relate in detail how Skinner saved Scindhia's life; how Scindhia presented him in durbar with golden bracelets and a Dekkanee charger; how, under Luckwa Dada, he took a splendid part in the wondrous siege of Jhajeeghur, and in the really terrific fight of Sanganeir, so bloody in one episode alone that even Skinner always spoke of it with horror—10,000 Rhattores sweeping in a dense body upon 8,000 men, and leaving only 200 alive behind them as they swept on; how they were magnificently fêted at Jeypore; and how Scindhia, puffed up by victory, began to alienate his allies by his senseless debaucheries, until one day, when in sight of the army of the Oonearah Rajah, his forces deserted him,

Skinner's troop alone remaining staunch. How in that splendid retreat Skinner was wounded and left upon the field with the corpses of over 900 of his 1,000 sowars ; how his life was saved by an old chumar woman who, " for the love of God," visited the battlefield on the next day with bread and water ; and how the Oonearah Rajah, with a fine chivalry, released Skinner with presents. How Perron, losing in his military pride all the virtues that had made him popular, fell from power ; how George Thomas, that phenomenon even among the adventurers of those days, fought with Perron, and after the defeat at Georgeghur cut his way with only 300 men through five battalions of the enemy, Skinner's Horse cheering him as he dashed away ; how, after the battle, Skinner and his brother heard each that the other was dead, and searched the whole night for each other's corpses ; and how, returning to report to the colonel, they entered at the same moment by opposite doors of the tent and met ; how, soon after, Scindhia fell out with the English, and the Skinners were dismissed, to their great disgust, from the Mahratta service.

For Skinner was a native in all but name, and cared only for the comrades and the colours with whom and under which he had passed so brilliant a career. So Skinner went to Allyghur, where Perron was preparing for Lord Lake, and begged to be taken back into the service. At Allyghur he pitched his tent in a garden, and hearing that battle was imminent, drew near to the probable scene of conflict ; but Perron had already been beaten, and Skinner saw him pass hatless and excited, one of a group of galloping horsemen. Skinner called out to him, and they met ; but Perron would not take him back. "Ah ! no," he said, " it is all over ; these fellows " (pointing to his Horse) " have behaved ill ; do not ruin yourselves : go over to the British ; it is all up with us." " By no means," said Skinner ; " let us rally ; you may depend on having many yet to fight for you." But

Perron still shook his head, and after a little, said in broken English, "Ah! no, Monsieur Skinner, I not trust you, I not trust you.   I afraid you all go."   Skinner on this got angry ; and as Perron rode off, roared out, " Then you may go to the devil ! "   He went himself to Lord Lake, and at Delhi was appointed to the command of the Yellow-coated Horse.

Such is briefly the history of the man whom Perron's troopers elected as their leader, and his first action under the British colours covered this fine Corps with glory.   In the Meerut district, about eight coss from Secundra, was the fort of Malaghur, held by Madharao the Mahratta, and from him Skinner received an order to quit the district. Skinner's reply provoked the chief to fight, and about a mile from Secundra the forces met.   Twice was Skinner repulsed in his attack ; but the third time, turning to his men with scorn and anger in his appeal, he stung them into fury, and more like devils than men the small band of the Yellow Troop dashed upon the strong position of the Mahratta chief, captured the guns, and cut down almost every man of the infantry.   (In this engagement Lieutenant Scott greatly distinguished himself, receiving no fewer than eleven sabre wounds.   For subsequent gallantry this fine soldier was individually thanked by the Commander-in-Chief, and promoted to the command of a Nujeeb force at Delhi.)

The Cavalry escaped to Malaghur, and within the fort were safe, until Skinner, learning that fodder was scarce for the many horses crowded within the defences, offered a reward to any man who would destroy the supply.   A man volunteered, and started on his perilous errand.   For two days nothing was heard of him, and it was feared he had perished, when one night he presented himself to Skinner.   " I have earned," he said, " the reward ; a slow match is now burning beneath each stack " ; and the words had hardly gone round the camp before the night sky was lit up by the flames of Malaghur.   The fort surrendered at once, Madharao was sent to Delhi, 600 of his sowars entered British service, and Captain Skinner was placed in general command of the country between Allyghur and Delhi, with a roving commission to secure tranquillity.

And hardly at any time in the history of our wars in India has the utility of Irregular Cavalry, its dash and devilry, been so illustrated as when Skinner held the country between Allyghur and Delhi. Brilliant above all his exploits was the sudden swoop upon the Sikhs at Saharunpore, when with 800 horse Skinner cut up 5,000 men, and brought back with him all the confederate chiefs who had assembled on the Jumna. For six months this restless soldier was occupied in fighting round Saharunpore, and was everywhere successful ; but in the following year the lesson he read from the chapter of chances was a bitter one.

At the Pass of Laswarree, the first Mahratta War had virtually ended, and Scindhia appears no more as the chief opponent of the British. But on the ruins of his misfortunes had risen the foundations of Holkar's fortunes, and against him now turned the tide of war.

General Monson was retiring in disgrace before Holkar, and Captain Skinner was ordered to raise his Corps to 1,200 horse and to join the detachment proceeding to his support. But Holkar's fame was terrible, and Skinner's newly recruited troopers began to desert. Opposite Muttra the panic reached its climax ; and from it resulted one of those picturesque episodes which can hardly be looked for but in the story of some such Corps as Skinner's Horse.

With the troops at this time was Lieutenant Robert Skinner, formerly in the service of the Begum Sombre ; and in command of six risalahs, this officer had crossed the river. Captain Skinner was on the other side with the remainder, when three risalahs, who had been ordered to cross, saddled their horses and galloped in the direction of the ford ; but there, thinking themselves out of sight, turned off when they had passed it, and rode towards Koonjah. Skinner was dumbfounded, and before he could make up his mind what to do in the emergency, he heard his khas risalah saddling their horses without orders ! The moment was one of intense anxiety ; but it was soon over, for with shouts his favourite troop came riding up, calling out to be led against the deserters who were disgracing the Corps. Then Skinner, leaping upon his horse, made the risalahs swear upon the Koran that they would follow where he led, and within the hour they had overtaken the runaways.

But not even their defiant attitude could persuade Skinner that his men were earnest in their desertion, so, advancing alone, he addressed them in the kindest language. But they would not return ; and, his anger rising, Skinner called them the cowards they were. Upon this several guns were fired at him, and Skinner fell. But the khas risalah were looking on, and when they saw their leader fall, they sent up a cry that rang along the country till the troops beyond the river heard it, and with the dash of tigers they came down upon the mutineers. Hardly a third of the runaways escaped to the fort of the Hattras Rajah to tell of the revenge of the Skinner's Horse.

Meanwhile Skinner himself was unhurt, for the fire of the renegades had only killed his horse, and next morning, with the remnant of his force, he joined the detachment. Lord Lake soon after arrived in camp and inspected the Corps of which he had heard so much, spoke in high terms of their gallantry on the field, increased the pay of the sowars, and directed four galloper guns to be permanently attached to the Corps.

Nevertheless, this desertion of his yellow boys was felt with keen bitterness by their gallant leader, who, in his reply to an attack made on his Corps by "A Bengal Cavalry

Officer," in the *Calcutta Review*, then edited by James Silk Buckingham, himself thus defends his Horse :

"After the affair I crossed the river, and during the interval vast numbers of soldiers, European officers and camp followers, belonging to the disastrous detachment of the Hon'ble Colonel Monson, came in daily, stript almost naked, many without their noses and hands, and in other respects in a miserable condition. The alarm occasioned in the detachment by the sight of these wretched men was very great, and I do not wish to describe it. Nevertheless my Corps continued to perform all the camp duties with alacrity, and as good soldiers should. The day before the detachment I was with commenced its retreat to Agra, fifty of my sowars, who were placed with the regulars at one of the pickets, deserted, and in this instance it would be necessary for the Bengal Cavalry officer to ascertain if my men alone went off, or if the regulars accompanied them. They commenced their march about seven o'clock in the evening, leaving me encamped as I was. A few hours afterwards, finding myself alone, I struck my camp and followed their route. I found many of their tents standing, and most of their baggage still lying on the ground. I kept in the rear with the little I had, and about daybreak brought it up safe to Furrah, which was half-way to Agra, without meeting with a single man of the enemy. I reported my arrival to the Commander-in-Chief, who thanked me for my exertions, and directed me to keep in the rear till the troops marched when the line halted for an hour or two. I then sat down with the officers of the 8th N.I., many of whom are now alive ; and I call upon them as well as the different commandants of the infantry battalions, especially Colonel Burrell, who, I believe, was in the rear of the line, as was Captain Welsh, now living. I would appeal to him, as he remained with my Corps from Furrah to Gao Ghat, a distance of about six coss, to witness the steady attachment shown by my men upon this most trying occasion. To the best of my recollection, about this period 1,000 Hindustanee Horse were entertained at or near Delhi, and placed under the command of British officers on the approach of Holkar's Brigade towards Delhi. The whole of these Hindustanees, with the exception of one ressalah, went over to the enemy, and my Corps was the only one left in the service."

And even had they deserted the disgrace would have been one shared by all the force, for the retreat of the British Army upon Agra was more disgraceful than Monson's. Desertion was the order of the day. Not only individuals but companies, whole wings, went off daily. The reports of Holkar's approach in overwhelming force caused a perfect panic, and, says Skinner, " the greatest confusion I ever witnessed prevailed." " The best of the business " (we quote Skinner again) " was, that Holkar was running off one way while we were running from him in another. The officers lost all their property ; and such was our fright and confusion, that I do not believe any Regiment could number twenty men under their colours. Had the detachment met 1,000 resolute men of the enemy, we should have made a worse business of it than Monson's. We pushed on to Agra, where we took shelter under the fort ; and so greatly was the character of the British troops degraded in the native eyes by our behaviour, that every thief pelted us all night with stones." For some time the Army remained *in situ*, refractory zemindars ensconced in mud forts affording Skinner's Horse the very exercise they loved. It was said of them that they looted ; but it was never denied that they fought like the bravest men, expecting no quarter and giving little.

But suddenly Lord Lake heard from the Resident at Delhi that Holkar, with a vast force, was before that place, and gave the orders for an advance on the threatened spot. But the Army was powerless to move ! A great convoy, which was bringing the supplies for the march, had been detained by the Hattras Rajah, and Skinner was at once deputed to rescue the convoy. Leaving his brother to follow with the remainder, Captain Skinner dashed on with 400 sowars, and reached Hattras in time to find the brinjaras unloading their cattle. Whip in hand, Skinner and a few of his Horse rode among the men of commerce, and compelled them to reload, and in a few hours, the immense convoy of 60,000 bullocks was in motion towards Lord Lake's camp. At this moment the Rajah of Hattras was seen to issue from the fort, and from the other side, a *deus ex machina*, appeared Robert Skinner with the remainder of the Corps. Seeing the reinforcement, the Rajah deemed it prudent, after firing a few shots, to hold a parley, which resulted in the Rajah retiring, in spite of the splendid loot the convoy offered. Captain Skinner conveyed his charge safely to Lord Lake's camp, and was presented by the Commander-in-Chief with his own sword, and Rs.20,000 were distributed among the sowars.

The convoy had brought a seven days' supply of grain for the whole army, so Lord Lake at once marched on Delhi. Holkar thereupon retired, halting in the territory of the Begum Sombre, to persuade her to join him against the British. Information of this was, however, carried to Lord Lake, who at once ordered Captain Skinner to advance, and ascertain its truth. The yellow boys had not gone far before they came upon an advance guard of Cavalry, which, after a severe engagement and great loss, Skinner repelled. The victory was hardly gained, however, before the main army of Holkar was discovered approaching, and the distinguished Corps whose career we are thus briefly recording would certainly have ceased to exist had it not happened that Lord Lake, anxious as to the fate of his Cavalry, had followed them up. The Armies were in sight of each other ; but there was yet time to recognise, as it deserved, the gallantry of Skinner's Horse, and halting the whole Army, Lord Lake drew from his holsters a pair of pistols, with which, on the site of his very gallant exploit, he presented Captain Skinner, the British Infantry applauding the graceful compliment paid to pluck by sending up a cheer that so alarmed Holkar that in an hour he was in full retreat to Futtehghur.

Lord Lake started in pursuit, came up with the force and inflicted severe loss. Deeming it rash to pursue further, Lord Lake halted, sending Captain Skinner in advance to follow Holkar up and watch his movements. Acting upon orders with their usual élan, the Yellow Troop appeared before Mynpoorie just as that place was about to surrender to Holkar, who retired precipitately on Skinner's appearance. And in this way, coming up with him at every halt, Skinner drove Holkar from Futtehghur to Mynpoorie, from Mynpoorie to Etah, from thence to Mahabun, through the Doab, and across the Jumna at Muttra. He then returned to headquarters.

During this brilliant pursuit the daily marches averaged thirty-one miles, the horses were seldom unsaddled, and the men slept every night under arms, subsisting during the day upon the green crops standing in the fields! Recognising, as it deserved, this fine exploit, Lord Lake gave Captain Skinner a fine horse with silver trappings, and dismissed him, with permission to halt at Coel to rest his exhausted Corps, at the same time authorising him to raise its strength to 1,700 horse. Before dismissing them, Lord Lake inspected the troop, and before all the forces complimented them upon their unvarying gallantry, adding the memorable words: " By your services you have established a claim for life on the British Government which shall never be forgotten, and your bread is made permanent."

The rest at Coel was, however, a very short one, for Skinner's Horse could not be spared; and in the action of Allygunge this Corps sustained its reputation. Meanwhile the Grand Army was before Bhurtpore, and the Yellow Troop was sent for, to keep communications open and to guard the grain convoys—on one of these occasions

distinguishing itself signally. A brinjara convoy, num-
bering no fewer than 100,000 bullocks, and heavily laden
with grain, was en route from Anoopahahur, and Skinner
was sent to escort it in. Having met it, Skinner dispersed
the greater part of his horsemen among the drovers, in
order to keep them from straying or deserting, and with
the remainder of his Horse protected their rear. At
Kamoona the convoy was attacked by Doondhia Khan,
but with only 400 of his men Captain Skinner repelled
and drove him back to the walls of his fort, inflicting a
loss upon his force of nearly half their number. The
convoy reached the Grand Army without a bullock
missing, an exploit for which the Yellow Troop was
publicly thanked by the Commander-in-Chief.

First Scindhia and then Holkar having been defeated,
Ameer Khan, the great Pathan adventurer, comes upon
the scene. After considerable success on the other side,
Ameer Khan crossed the Jumna. The siege of Kamoona
was at once raised, and Colonel Gruber retired under the
the walls of Allyghur, where General Smith came to his
assistance, Skinner's Horse distinguishing themselves in
the advance by cutting up to a man a " ghole " of 300
sowars. After this the yellow boys were ordered to
Bareilly, where Ameer Khan's troops were besieging Mr.
Leicester, and with much gallantry they effected their
mission. But Ameer Khan himself was impossible to
catch. He was a veritable will-o'-the-wisp, and kept
the whole Army marching backward and forward for a
long time.

At last Skinner discovered his real direction, and volunteered to General Smith to go in disguise to the enemy's
camp and learn his intentions. Accordingly, putting on
native dress, Skinner, taking ten faithful sowars with him
and giving out that he was going to Moorshedabad on
private business, started for Sherekote, and falling in
with some of Ameer Khan's foragers, accompanied them
into camp. Next day Skinner found that the enemy had

fallen out, and the forces of Ameer Khan, Pindarees on the one side, Pathans on the other, ranged themselves for battle. Seizing the opportunity, Skinner escaped from the camp, and urged General Smith to advance. The army at once struck its tents ; but Ameer Khan had already got scent of the movement, and the British force came up with him only at Ufzulghur. The fight was a very bloody one, but the triumph complete.

As the Army was retiring, it was seen that one of Skinner's galloper guns was left unprotected, and about fifty of Ameer Khan's sowars dashed out to capture it. They had all but secured it, when Lieutenant Robert Skinner, with twenty of his men, proceeded to its rescue, in personal combat cut down the leader of the enemy, and brought back the gun. This very gallant action was performed in the sight of the whole British Force, and as Lieutenant Skinner rode into the line, he was cheered by the British Dragoons. For its conduct throughout this affair, Skinner's Horse was again thanked by Lord Lake ; and General Smith was instructed to present a sword to Captain Skinner.

But this incidental mention of Lieutenant Robert Skinner reminds us that we do his gallant memory a grave injustice in not enumerating in more detail his very brilliant acts of bravery. In every action in which he was engaged he personally distinguished himself, on several occasions had his horse shot under him, and at Ufzulghur, as we have seen above, behaved with very conspicuous gallantry. But it is with Sumbhul that the name of Robert Skinner is most gloriously connected. Ameer Khan had been chased to Mooradabad, and from there across the Ramgunga, towards, it was supposed, Bareilly. But after the affair of Ufzulghur, Robert Skinner had been despatched, with a detachment of 500 horse, to Anoopahahur, and at Sumbhul he was suddenly surprised by the whole Army of Ameer Khan, who, with his magical activity, had doubled upon his pursuers, and

Skinner's troopers were compelled to take shelter in an
old fortified serai.

Ameer Khan first tried to bribe Skinner's men to betray
their commandant, but they received his offers with
contempt.   Ameer Khan then attempted to storm the serai,
but was repulsed with loss.   Again the disgraceful over-
tures were made, but the native officers brought the letter
to Lieutenant Skinner, who put their fidelity to the test.
" If," he said, " by giving up one life, that of five hundred
can be saved, I am willing to go as prisoner to Ameer Khan";
and their reply, which should be blazoned on the banners
of the Corps, was this : " You may go after we have all
been killed."   Skinner then wrote to Ameer Khan,
taunting him with his vile conduct, and the result was a
prolonged attack upon the serai, but with no success.

Bent, however, upon the massacre of the brave detachment, Ameer Khan continued his attack, until Skinner was
reduced to fearful straits.   Of food there was hardly any,
of powder very little, and of ammunition none.   The
shoes were taken off the horses' feet, and slugs made from
the metal.   At the same time a messenger was despatched
to Captain Skinner to apprise him of the desperate situation
of his brother, and to ask for reinforcements.   But General
Smith would not allow him to proceed to his assistance,
arguing that by this time either every man of the detachment was dead or that Ameer Khan had been defeated by
Colonel Burne's force, which was in the neighbourhood.

Captain Skinner, helpless to render assistance to his
brother in his distress, determined to attempt strategy, and
gloriously succeeded.   He wrote a letter to Robert Skinner,
saying that General Smith had ordered the whole Army
to move to his assistance, and that he would be relieved
on the following morning ; at the same time urging him
to keep Ameer Khan amused before the walls, in order
that his defeat might be complete.   This letter was given
to a messenger with instructions to fall into the hands of
Ameer Khan's vedettes ; and the gallant fellow carried

out his instructions well, for he allowed himself to be captured by an outpost and carried before Ameer Khan. The letter was found upon him and read, and great was the consternation in the camp. The whole British Army was within a night's march ! The order was at once given to strike the tents ; but before the Army could move, a village in the rear was seen to burst into flame, and the country-people, rushing into the camp, declared that Lord Lake was already upon them, for the Yellow Troop was firing the villages. The truth was that a few sowars had volunteered to assist Captain Skinner in carrying out his ruse, and, by opportunely firing the village, had corroborated the alarming letter received by Ameer Khan. The terror of the Pathan was, however, complete, for he fled in confusion from before Sumbhul, leaving Robert Skinner and his gallant men as astonished as delighted to make their way from the serai to the British camp in perfect safety.

The messenger who carried the letter and the sowars who assisted the stratagem were handsomely rewarded ; and Robert Skinner and his detachment were specially thanked by the Commander-in-Chief, who sent a letter in Persian to the Regiment, applauding them for the gallantry of their defence and the severe loss they had inflicted upon Ameer Khan ; and thus ended this wonderful campaign.

In the chase after Holkar the Army had gone 500 miles, after Ameer Khan 700, and Skinner's Horse was the only Hindustanee Corps that was in active service throughout. During the whole time the men were eighteen hours out of the twenty-four in the saddle ; and often in the chase after Ameer Khan, when they had the rear-guard, they picked up the European Dragoons knocked up, and, themselves dismounting, put them on their horses and brought them into camp. And thus it was that " the Yellow Boys " were as popular among their friends as dreaded by their enemies.

Ameer Khan by this time had crossed the Jumna, a

ruined man in reputation, without an army, and without means. No enemies now remained for the British to fight. The times grew wearily peaceful, for Scindhia and Holkar both pretended to come to terms, and at last came the order for the break-up of the force with which Skinner's Horse was serving. Captain Skinner, on his way to Saharunpore, passed through Delhi, and here Colonel Ochterlony, the British Resident, inspected the Corps, and after thanking it for its distinguished services, unbuckled his own sword, and in the name of Lord Lake presented it to Captain Skinner.

But very soon Holkar, with Ameer Khan's shattered forces, started for Lahore, marching through the Hurriana country, to enlist the assistance of Runjeet Singh, and in 1805 Lord Lake, re-forming the Army, started in pursuit. At the Sutlej, the opinions of the military and political authorities (Sir John Malcolm) clashed as to the propriety of crossing into the territory of Ranjeet Singh ; but Lord Lake, taking the responsibility upon himself, ordered the Yellow Boys to lead the way across the river. Captain Skinner made a short speech to his men, who with three cheers dashed into the river. The horses swam for a short distance, and then, feeling the bottom, scrambled on to an island in the middle of the river. It proved, however, to be a quicksand, so, cutting the fastenings of the galloper gun which they had taken with them, Captain Skinner ordered his men to proceed. They reached the shore ; and then, having picketed the horses, returned, and in sight of the Lord Lake, his Staff, and a number of officers who had assembled to see the achievement, rescued the gun from the treacherous sand, and as it touched the firm soil, Skinner, taking off his hat, gave three cheers, in which Lord Lake and his Staff joined, to proclaim the fact that a British gun had crossed the Sutlej. So pleased was Lord Lake at the manner in which this work was performed, that he ordered Rs.2,000 to be given to the men who went over with the gun.

2

Holkar, however, was far in advance ; and as the only chance of inflicting any loss upon him, Lord Lake ordered Captain Skinner to pursue him alone.   At the Beas River the Yellow Boys found Holkar crossing, and, after cutting up the detachment which had not yet passed across, captured a large convoy of grain and brought it back to Lord Lake ; that is to say, after marching twenty miles with the Army, Skinner's Horse advanced ten miles alone, cut up the rear-guard of Holkar's Army, captured a convoy and brought it into camp, having been absent about fifteen hours, and then proceeded with the Regular Army on its march as if it had never left it !

When Lord Lake reached the Beas, he found Holkar ready to sue for peace ; and after holding a grand review, at which Ranjeet Singh was himself present in disguise, and which Sikhs to this day remember as the exhibition of a strength then undreamt of by them, turned homewards. At Kurnaul the Army was broken up ; and though Skinner's Horse had been promised by Lord Lake permanent service, Sir George Barlow ordered the whole Corps to be dismissed. When Skinner arrived, Lord Lake was at breakfast ; but he was sent for, and, with tears in his eyes, his Lordship gave him the despatch from Sir George Barlow.   " I read it " (we quote Skinner's own narrative) " but said nothing ; when Lord Lake, catching my hand, said, ' Skinner, I am very sorry indeed for it ; what can I do for you ? ' ' My Lord,' I replied, ' the character you have given me will enable me to earn my bread, and some just man may hereafter come to the head of affairs who will take me by the hand.' ' Well,' said Lord Lake, ' but how can I satisfy you now ? '   I replied that I should be content with a small jagheer, as I did not mean to serve again as a soldier unless obliged.   He asked me how much would satisfy me and my brother Robert—would Rs.20,000 a year satisfy us ?   I thanked him, and said he was making princes of us.   Lord Lake laughed, and appointed jagheers of Rs.5,000 a year apiece to four of my ressaldars, pensioned all officers as low as duffadars, gave three months' gratuity to all the men, and placed the sick and wounded upon the Haupper establishment.   I then took my leave, with a letter to the Collector of Coel for jagheers ; and, returning, brought the Corps to Delhi, where the painful task awaited me of tearing myself from the men who had gained such laurels under the British colours. All those who had deserted that service at first, and then come over to it, received rewards. Those only who had proved faithful all along were discharged from it."

These are bitter words ; but Skinner meant them as he wrote, and to this day they remain true.   But worse was yet to come, for Sir George Barlow cancelled the order of Skinner's jagheers, on the plea that, being British subjects, they could not hold land !   At Delhi the Yellow Boys met, and Captain Skinner paid up his veterans and discharged them, settling himself at that place upon a Captain's pension.

The strength of Skinner's Corps at the termination of the war was 1,700.   When it was broken up, the whole of this force was disbanded, with the exception of Skinner's own Bargheers, mounted on his own horses.   This miserable termination to a most brilliant career was not, however, to be, for when the Sikhs threatened trouble, Captain Skinner was ordered to raise his numbers to 800.   With this force and a couple of galloper guns, Captain Skinner proceeded, in 1809, to the Hurriana country, where for five years they did their usual excellent service in dashing about the country and suppressing turbulent raiders.

CHAPTER II

1814–1819

2ND AND 3RD CORPS RAISED—BHAWANEE—THE PINDARI
WAR—2ND CORPS DETACHED TO NEEMUCH—3RD CORPS
DISBANDED.

IN 1814 the state of the country called for an increase in
the number of Cavalry in the Bengal Army. Only a few
of the Regular Bengal Light Cavalry Regiments had been
raised up to now, and there were only three Irregular
Corps of the Skinner's Horse type. On the 6th December
1814 the Adjutant-General wrote from Moradabad to
Captain James Skinner, as he then was, saying that the
Governor-General, Lord Moira, had decided to increase
the strength of his Corps to 3,000 sowars. Skinner was
asked if he could collect the right stamp of man, and
whether he did not think he could draw off men from the
refractory chief Ameer Khan's following by the better
conditions of service offered by the " H.E.I.C." The
following is a copy of Skinner's reply :

*From James Skinner, Captain Commanding, Irregular
Horse, to Lieutenant-Colonel G. H. Fagan, Adjutant-General.*

HANSI,
6th January 1815.

SIR,

I have the honor to acknowledge the receipt of
your Public Letter dated 7th December 1814, communi-
cating to me the pleasure of the Right Honorable the
Commander-in-Chief to increase the number of the Corps
under my Command to 3,000 sowars.

I am unable to express sufficiently to you my sense of
the honour thus conferred upon me by the Government,

as well as for the gratifying assurance of their confidence in my loyalty and courage.

I beg leave to say it will ever be the study of my life to merit their approbation by a zealous and faithful discharge of my duty and entire devotion to the Service of the British Government.

I enclose herewith a Present State of the Recruits already entertained.

I have, etc.

(Signed) JAMES SKINNER,
Captain Commanding,
Irregular Horse.

Again on the 3rd February 1815 he wrote to the Adjutant-General:

" I am happy to inform you that my Corps was completed on the 29th January 1815.   Horsemen are still coming in daily from all quarters, and I am now discharging the bad ones and taking in good.   All those that come from Meer Khan's Camp are very good Horsemen."

It was not until July of the same year that an establishment and the organisation of Skinner's Command into three Corps of 1,000 sowars each was published in G.O.C.C.s.

The following warrant fixes the official birthday of the 2nd Corps as 7th December 1814.

From John Adam, Esquire, Secretary to Government, Secret Department, to Lieutenant-Colonel G. H. Fagan, Adjutant-General.

G.O.C.C. 29*th July* 1815.

The Corps of Irregular Cavalry under the Command of Lieutenant-Colonel James Skinner to be augmented to an Establishment of 3,000 sowars under authority conveyed to His Excellency the Commander-in-Chief in India, letter dated 7th December 1814.

Skinner recruited locally from the Harriana District and the Doab, and the majority were Moghuls and Sayids with a few Rajputs and Brahmans, but there was a place for any adventurer, and this attracted both Pathans and Baluchis.   The raising and training of a Regiment in those days was not the laborious process it now is, and it will be noted that Skinner was able to report on the 29th January 1815, that he had recruited his Corps up to strength, though the order to do so had only been issued on the 6th December.   The Corps was recruited on what is known as the " Silladar System."   This was a very convenient and economical method of raising an Irregular Corps.   No initial outlay by Government was necessary, the men came with their own arms, equipment, and horses, and received a fixed sum a month for their services.   A Corps raised on this principle could be reduced or disbanded when no longer required, without the elaborate machinery of a Demobilisation Department or a Ministry of Pensions. The only training necessary was movement in formed bodies, as every able-bodied man in those days, who could afford to buy himself arms, was skilled in their use, and individual training did not go much beyond tent-pegging and shooting at bottles at the gallop.   The Corps was organised in " Risalahs " of 100 men each, equivalent to the " Troop " of the Regular Cavalry of that time.

One of the first questions that arose, and which may be taken as the first step in regularising the Irregular, was determining the status of British officers employed with these Corps.   Of the five officers employed with Skinner's Horse only one, Fraser, of the Civil Service, appears to have been in Government employ, the remainder were as irregular as their men and did not hold the King's Commission.   Robert Skinner became discontented with his position, and sent in his resignation.   The Governor-General, Lord Moira, took up the case with much sympathy, and wrote personally to the elder Skinner on the subject. He pointed out the obvious objections that would be raised by regular officers if officers of Irregular Corps were given commissions with the rank and seniority of the appointments they were holding in Irregular Corps, and asked Skinner to suggest how his brother could be reconciled, as he was particularly anxious not to lose the services of such men as the Skinners. James wished to separate a portion of his Corps to make an independent command for his younger brother, but the Governor-General could not agree to this : " What influences me in this decision," he said, " is the desire to keep your Command as respectable as possible, and I would prefer your brother to remain second to you with advanced rank, and I would be prepared to station a part of your command at a distance from your headquarters under his command."

The following arrangement was then decided upon. Officers of Irregular Corps were to be given local rank, but Captains of the Regular Army were to be senior to all Captains of Irregular Corps. Field Officers of Irregular Corps, would, however, command Captains of the Regular Army. James Skinner was given the local rank of Lieutenant-Colonel, and Robert that of Major. When later it became the practice to second Regular officers for service with these Irregular Corps, this difficulty disappeared. The majority of officers posted to Irregular Cavalry were drawn from Native Infantry Regiments.

Colonel Skinner had, of course, supreme command of his three Corps. Robert Skinner is shown in the Army List of that date as second-in-command, but nominally held command of the 2nd Corps. The 3rd Corps was commanded by Major Fraser, who was afterwards murdered at Delhi at the instigation of the Nawab Sham-Shud-Din.

Major Fraser's career was somewhat unique—a characteristic page in the early history of the English in India. He was in reality a civilian who had held very high political appointments under Lord Hastings's Goverment. With a great talent for administration and diplomacy he united a brilliant dash and vigour of character, which eminently qualified him for the command of Irregular Cavalry. The Governor-General's keen and ready insight into character was not slow to recognise these qualities. He saw in Mr. Fraser the material for a leader of horse, and a leader of horse he accordingly made him, giving him the rank of Major, and permitting him, on all occasions of active service, to join Skinner's Regiment (in which he had already distinguished himself as a volunteer), and allowing him to revert at other times to his substantive appointment—Chief Commissioner of the Ceded Provinces.

As early as the hot weather of 1815, Skinner was employed with his newly raised Corps against the refractory town of Bhawanee, a large fortified village near Hansi. In this action the Corps greatly distinguished itself by charging the garrison as it attempted to escape.

The Nepaulese, or Ghurka War, afforded but few and imperfect opportunities for the use of horse. Small detachments of Skinner's Horse were attached to columns employed against the Ghurkas, as at Kalunga and Jytock. Detachments were also employed with columns in overawing the powers of Hindustan, especially Scindhia and Holkar, who were looking anxiously to the event of our contest with the Nepaulese, and who, upon the unsuccessful opening of that war, showed very significant symptoms of the spirit that animated them. The necessity for the increase of the numbers of Irregular Cavalry was due to the enterprise which had for some time been contemplated by the Marquis of Hastings against the Pindaris, who had become the pest of the country.

In December 1817 three large columns were assembled in Northern India to co-operate with columns from the south against the Pindaris under Ameer Khan and Appa Sahib, the ex-Rajah of Nagpur. The 1st and 2nd Corps joined the right wing, which assembled at Delhi under Sir David Ochterlony, for operations in Rajputana and Malwa. The 3rd Corps was left at Hansi for the protection of that district. During this campaign the 1st Corps was placed under the command of Major-General Sir John Malcolm, commanding in Malwa, who detached it to escort Bajie Rao to Baitool.   The 2nd Corps, under Robert Skinner, was placed under the orders of Lieutenant-Colonel Smith ; this Corps greatly distinguished itself in an affray with the Appa Sahib whom Robert Skinner charged and pursued to the very gates of the Aseerghur.   Later it escorted Chinumun, Bajie Rao's brother, to Allahabad.

In a letter from Major-General Sir John Malcolm to the Adjutant-General, it says :

" It would be indeed unjust not to bring to the notice of His Excellency the Most Noble the Commander-in-Chief, the manner in which Skinner's Horse continued to perform every duty entrusted to them, and particularly in those escort parties on which they are chiefly employed. I cannot give a stronger proof of this than by stating that there has not for two years been a complaint against one man, either from the officers detaching them or from the inhabitants of the country they are constantly traversing."

By the end of 1819 both Corps had returned to their Headquarters at Hansi ; here Skinner received orders to disband the 3rd Corps, and detach the 2nd Corps under Robert Skinner to Neemuch where it would be permanently stationed.   This was in accordance with the previous arrangements made by the Governor-General with James Skinner to allow Robert Skinner an independent command.

The history of Skinner's Horse from this point is that of the 1st and 2nd Corps, and must be recorded separately. These two Corps never served together again under Skinner's command, except for a short period in 1838, when they were formed into a Cavalry Brigade in the Army of the Indus which had been assembled at Ferozepore for operations against Afghanistan.

PART II

THE 1st CORPS OR THE 1st DUKE OF YORK'S OWN LANCERS (SKINNER'S HORSE)

" Bhurtpore " ; " Candahar, 1842 "; "Afghanistan, 1879–80 "; " Pekin, 1900 "; " The Great War " ; " North-West Frontier, 1915 " ; " Third Afghan War."

Extract from Bengal Army List 1823

LOCAL CAVALRY

1ST REGIMENT (OR SKINNER'S) LOCAL HORSE

Hansi

Rank and Names.	Army Rank.	Remarks.
Local Lieutenant-Colonel James Skinner	—	Commandant.
Local Lieutenant William Martindell	30 Sept. 1817	Second in Command.
Local Lieutenant R. Grueber .	12 Sept. 1823	Adjutant.
Local Cornet J. M. Turnbull .	19 June 1819	—
Mr. C. Ray	—	Assistant Surgeon.

CHAPTER III

1819–1841

IN 1820 the Corps was reduced to its peace establishment of 800 men, to be again increased in 1821 to 1,000, at which time Skinner was also ordered to raise a new Corps 1,000 strong, which was known as the 8th Local Horse. Both these Corps served with the British Army during the second siege of Bhurtpore in 1825–26, covering the communications, and on foraging and convoy duties. Mention may be made of a most gallant affair at Konheir, when two Risalahs of the 1st Skinner's Horse, under Risaldars Amanat Khan and Zabberdast Khan, engaged upwards of 1,000 of the enemy's horse under some well-known leaders. In spite of the difference in numbers the enemy were completely routed with very heavy loss. The Commander-in-Chief issued an order, commending the two Risaldars for their bold decision and gallant execution of it, and praising the conduct of all ranks engaged. Risaldar Amanat Khan was a Pathan of Sewli, District Gurgaon ; Zabberdast Khan (Pathan) a son of Jemadar Pir Bakhsh Khan, one of the first of Skinner's soldiers, another of whom was Risaldar Imam Ali Khan, grand-uncle of Nawab Ibrahim Ali Khan, present chief of Maler Kotla. Among the descendants of Zabberdast Khan there were serving in 1908, Ressaidar Ghulam Kadar Khan, Dafadar Ghaus Muhammad Khan, Dafadar Walidad Khan, Lance-Dafadar Bahawal Khan, and Sowar Muhammad Newaz Khan. Another incident was that of a picquet of the 1st Skinner's Horse, under Risaldar Mir Bahadur Ali, which charged a force of the enemy 250

strong, and put them to flight with a loss of thirty killed
and many wounded and prisoners. Lord Combermere,
the Commander-in-Chief, directed that his thanks should
be conveyed to all those who took part in the skirmish.
Risaldar Mir Bahadur Ali was a Sayed of Kharkhauda,
District Rohtak, and was originally enlisted as a Risaldar
with a troop of his own men in the Regiment. This fine
soldier, having given proofs of his loyalty and gallantry
on many occasions in the field, was killed at Dhadar during
the first Afghan War. After the capture of Bhurtpore,
the Commander-in-Chief expressed his approbation of the
services of Skinner's Horse, stating that " nothing could
exceed the devotion and courage of this valuable class of
soldier."   His thanks were also conveyed to the following
officers, who volunteered for the actual assault—Risaldar
Muhammad Shadal Khan, Ressaidar Adal Khan, and
Naib Ressaidars Chaund Khan, and Sandal Khan.   It
should be mentioned that when 200 volunteers from the
Regiment were called for, the whole Regiment volunteered,
and Skinner was obliged to select 200 men according to
roster next for duty.   Skinner himself received the C.B.,
and, in order to qualify him for this, it was necessary to
make him a substantive Lieutenant-Colonel in the British
Army.   This finally settled the question of his rank and
seniority in the Army, which had been a source of bitter
resentment to him.   He was also granted the local rank
of Brigadier.

Some years of peace followed, during which the Corps
was stationed principally at Hansi.   In 1832 the Governor-
General made a tour through Rajputana, to settle many
important points with the Chiefs of that district.   At his
special request, Lieutenant-Colonel Skinner and a large
portion of his Corps accompanied the Governor-General,
Lord William Bentinck, who made great use of Skinner's
knowledge of and influence with the local Chiefs and
Sirdars, who had been both his comrades and his opponents
in the field.   Among these was Meer Khan, previously

mentioned, from whom, as from others, Skinner received many marks of esteem and regard.

At the conclusion of the tour, Sir William Bentinck presented Lieutenant-Colonel Skinner with a vase inscribed with an appreciation of his services, and also reported that among the large number of officers not belonging to the Regular Army, none had distinguished himself so long or so well, as a loyal and gallant soldier in all military operations, as Colonel Skinner, and he also spoke of the devotion and gallantry of his Corps, which had been so abundantly proved on so many occasions in the presence of the enemies of the British Raj.

There now succeeded a long period of peace. As Skinner said, " soldiering was over." The duties of his Corps consisted of nothing more than the occasional chastising of some robber band or refractory zemindar.

Towards the end of 1838, the Army of the Indus was assembled at Ferozepore for operations against Afghanistan. The 1st and 2nd Corps were formed into the 2nd Cavalry Brigade under Brigadier James Skinner. The story of the first phase of the first Afghan War is told in the history of the 2nd Corps. The Army of the Indus was reduced before it left Ferozepore and Skinner's Brigade broken up. The 2nd Corps and one Risalah of the 1st Corps marched with the Army to Kandahar. A Detachment of the 1st Corps was employed in Scinde against the Baluchis under the Khan of Kelat, and formed, with two guns and three companies of Bombay Infantry, the Garrison of Dhadar Khan, near the entrance to the Bolan.

On the 28th October 1840, the Baluchis to the number of 9,000 debouched from the pass and encamped four miles from the Cantonment. Next day about noon their guns opened on our troops, and some 4,000 men advanced to the attack. They were met by the fire of our six-pounders, which, though it caused considerable loss, did not stop their advance, and the enemy, keeping up a hot fire, got to within 250 yards of the position.

Extract from Bengal Army List " July 1839 "
LOCAL CAVALRY
1st REGIMENT OF LOCAL HORSE

Headquarters and 3 Rissalahs at Hansi.   2 Rissalahs on duty at Lood-
hianah, 5 Rissalahs on detached duties.

" Bhurtpoor."

Rank and Names.	Army Rank.	When appointed.	Remarks.
Colonel James Skin- ner, C.B.　.　.	18 June 1831	—	Commandant.
Local Lieutenant Wm. Martindell .	—	30 Sept. 1817	Second in Command.
Local Lieutenant Jas. Skinner, Jun.	—	18 Feb. 1825	Adjutant.
Local Lieutenant Jas. Turnbull .	—	18 Feb. 1825	Supernumerary.
Assistant Surgeon J. A. Staig . .	10 Jan. 1837	8 Feb. 1839	In medical charge.
Ressaldar Mirzah Azeem Beg .	1 May 1837	—	Sardar Bahadur.

The detachment of the 1st Corps, 120 sabres under
Captain Macpherson, was ordered to charge. At this
point the enemy had 600 horsemen, and some 1,500 footmen, many of the latter hidden in the thick cotton fields.
The enemy's horsemen fled as our own men advanced, but
the footmen stood their ground. They were, however,
overthrown with a loss of thirty-five killed and many
wounded, and the remainder beat a hasty retreat and took
cover among the buildings in cantonments. On our side
Captain Macpherson was wounded and Risaldar Mir
Bahadur and two sowars, Azizuddin and Karam Khan
of Kharkhauda, killed ; 2 native officers, 6 non-commissioned officers, and 18 men wounded, and 8 horses
killed and 20 wounded. The enemy maintained a hot
fire from the buildings in the cantonments until midnight,
for our guns could do them no damage after it had got
dark. During the night the enemy tried to rush our
position, but were driven off by steady fire.

It took two days for the enemy to make up his mind to

attack again, and when he did attack, it was with largely increased numbers. They approached to a point 350 yards from our position and opened a heavy fire on our men, causing many casualties. As our muskets could not carry that distance, our men were ordered to lie down under cover, till they approached within 50 yards. The brunt of the attack fell on the detachment of the 1st Corps, who held a mud wall enclosing the Agency compound. The enemy, however, did not venture on a nearer approach. The detachment had one native officer and four men wounded this day. Next day the detachment was reinforced by some levies, who fought steadily and bravely, and the enemy got no nearer, but they gained possession of the town, which they looted and burned, our force being insufficient to do more than maintain their position on the outskirts of cantonments.

When relief in the form of reinforcements arrived, the Officer Commanding not only reported on the gallant and steady conduct of the detachment of the 1st Corps in action, but also specially brought to notice their soldier-like conduct on 2nd November, when the reinforcements arrived. He said : " The men of all other Corps had dispersed to plunder, but the men of the 1st Corps, with the old Risaldar at their head, were standing ready for an instantaneous charge, should the enemy appear."

The " old Risaldar " was Ghulam Muhammad Khan, alias " Gul Khan," a Pathan of Lohari (District Muzaffarnagar). He and Naib Risaldar Muhammad Hussain Khan, who were cousins of Risaldar Ali Ahmad Khan, had come to the Regiment in its early days. A descendant of Muhammad Hussain Khan was Ressaidar Mobarak Ali Khan, who retired in 1891.

On the 4th December 1841 James Skinner died at Hansi, at the age of sixty-three. He had received a valuable jaghir in the Aligarh District, but he lived mainly at George Thomas's old capital of Hansi, where his

3

descendants still reside. He made a host of friends and found many admirers, amongst them such distinguished men as Lord Lake, Sir John Malcohn, Lord Metcalfe, Lord Minto, the Marquis of Hastings, Lord Combermere, and Lord William Bentinck. It is a goodly roll of patrons and acquaintances for the offspring of a Company's ensign and a Rajputnee girl, and one whose only introduction to high society was his own sterling worth.

Many anecdotes are related of Skinner, but only two or three can be recorded here. Perhaps his most remarkable characteristic was his modesty and utter contempt of all assumption. To the end of his life an old spoon was placed on his breakfast table every morning to remind him of his own humble origin and early days. In fulfilment of the vow he made on the battlefield of Uniara, to build a church to the God of his father if his life were spared, he erected the edifice of St. James at Delhi, at a cost of £20,000, and in the same spirit of modest humility before noted, often expressed a desire that when he died he should be buried, not within it, but under the door sill, so that all persons entering might trample upon " the chief of sinners."

Skinner's domestic habits were in some respects more Mohammedan than Christian, and he left behind him a numerous family by sundry wives, of whom he had at least fourteen. His eldest son, Hercules Skinner, was educated in England, and through the influence of Lord William Bentinck received a Commission in the Hyderabad Contingent, much to his father's delight. In 1836 Skinner was confirmed, and during his latter years was sincerely pious, constantly studying the Bible, and preparing himself for his end.

He was buried at Hansi with full military honours, but a little later his remains were disinterred, and carried to Delhi to be deposited by the side of his dearly loved comrade, William Fraser (brother to his biographer), under the altar of St. James's Church. It had been his wish to be buried near Fraser, and it was felt proper that this wish should be fulfilled.

On the 17th February 1842, accompanied by the whole of his Corps, and a great concourse of people, the coffin was carried from Hansi to Sitaram-ka-Sarai, on the outskirts of Delhi.   Here all that was mortal of the gallant old adventurer was met by the civilian and military officers of the station, and a vast multitude from the city, and so escorted to its final resting-place.   " None of the Emperors of Hindustan," said the natives, " were ever brought into Delhi in such state as Sikander Sahib."

It was thought at the time that Skinner's second son James, who had been Adjutant of the Corps, would succeed him in Command, but it was given to Brevet-Major Horton-Smith.   The head of his family, however, has always held a honorary commission in the Regiment.

Extract from Bengal Army List " July 1844 "

IRREGULAR CAVALRY

1st REGIMENT OF IRREGULAR CAVALRY

Neemuch, arrived 20th March 1843. Detachment at Ajmere.
" Bhurtpoor." Detachment " Candhar 1842."

Rank, Names, and Corps.	Army Rank.	When Appointed.	Remarks.
Major L. H. Smith, 6th L.C. . .	28 June 1838	23 Feb. 1842	Commandant—Leave, P.A., to 15th Jan. 1845.
Captain R. Haldane, 45th N.I. . .	17 June 1839	14 Nov. 1840	Second in Command.
Lieutenant T. Watson, 33rd N.I. .	24 Jan. 1840	11 Jan. 1844	Adjutant.
Assistant Surgeon J. A. Staig . .	10 Jan. 1837	8 Feb. 1839	—
Resaldar Mirzah Azeem Beg .	—	1 May 1837	Sardar Bahadur.

The 1st Regiment of Irregular Cavalry consists of 10 Ressallahs, with 1 Woordee Major, 1 Nakeeb, 2 native doctors, 1 English writer, 1 Persian writer, 5 Ressaldars, 5 Ressaidars, 10 Naib Ressaldars, 10 Jemadars, 10 Kote Duffadars, 90 Duffadars, 10 Nishanburdars, 5 Trumpeters, 5 Nuggarchies, 850 Sowars.

CHAPTER IV

1841–1857

In 1840 the designation of Regiments of Local Horse was changed to Irregular Cavalry, and the Regiment now became the 1st Irregular Cavalry.

When the news of the disastrous retreat from Kabul reached India in 1842, the headquarters of the Regiment was at Neemuch, one Risalah was already with General Nott at Kandahar, and two Risalahs in Scinde. These latter were at once ordered to Kandahar to join General Nott's command.

The following is a list of the Indian officers that served with the Detachment at Kandahar :

Risaldar Mirza Azim Beg of Delhi.
Risaldar Mir Madad Ali of Kharkhauda.
Risaldar Shekh Ghulam Hassain of Hansi.
Risaldar Ghulam Ali of Hansi.
Risaldar Ramzam of Hansi.
Naib Risaldar Rustam Khan of Lohari.
Naib Risaldar Babar Khan of Lohari.
Naib Risaldar Karam Khan of Lohari.
Naib Risaldar Jamal Khan of Jhajjar.
Naib Risaldar Kamruddin Khan of Bara Basti.
Jemadar Mir Tajuddin of Kharkhauda.

Very heavy and severe fighting ensued around Kandahar in which the Detachment took part, and in consequence the Regiment was permitted to bear the inscription : " KANDAHAR 1842 " on its colours.

The total casualties of the Detachment were 108 men killed in action and died of disease out of a total of 180 all ranks—a sufficient proof of the severity of the service in which they had been engaged.

It was not till August 1842 that General Nott received permission to advance on Kabul. He reached it on the 17th September—just two days after the arrival there of General Pollock's Army from the Khyber. After inflicting punishment on the city of Kabul, the evacuation of Afghanistan began, and on the 12th October 1842 the return march to India, via Jelalabad was commenced. The Detachment joined the Regiment at Neemuch.

On the outbreak of the first Sikh War in 1845, the Regiment was ordered from Neemuch to the front, but the campaign was brought to an end just as the Regiment reached Hansi. The Regiment then returned to Neemuch, where it remained till 1849, when it marched to Lahore. In this year Major Smith resigned and Lieutenant Crawford Chamberlain was appointed to the command.

In 1852 the Regiment marched to Peshawar, and, in December, troops sent out in view of an expected attack on Shubkadr had a sharp skirmish with hill-men, in which their leader Painder Khan, was killed and the enemy dispersed.

In 1854 a similar action was fought near Michni against the Mohmands, for which the Frontier Medal was given.

In this year the Regiment moved in relief to Jhelum and in 1857 to Multan, which was reached on the 4th April.

Extract from Bengal Army List 1857

18 *REGIMENTS OF IRREGULAR CAVALRY*

1st IRREGULAR CAVALRY

Jhelum, arrived 11th January 1856
" Bhurtpoor."   Detachment : " Candahar 1842."

Rank, Names, and Corps.	Army Rank.	When Appointed.	Remarks.
Major C. T. Chamberlain, 28th N.I..	2 May 1852	19 Nov. 1849	Commandant.
1st Lieutenant R. J. F. Hickey, 1st En. B.F. . . .	17 June 1848	27 Oct. 1855	Second in Command.
Lieutenant C. C. Ekins, 20th N.I. .	1 Jan. 1851	Aug. 1855	Adjutant.
Assistant Surgeon J. D. Crawford, AB and MB .	11 Aug. 1846	5 Oct. 1850	—

The 1st Regiment of Irregular Cavalry consists of 6 Ressallahs, with 2 native doctors, 3 Ressaldars, 3 Ressaidars, 6 Naib Ressaldars, 6 Jemadars, 6 Kote Duffadars, 48 Duffadars, 6 Nishanburdars, 3 Trumpeters, 3 Nuggarchies, 500 Sowars.

The 2nd, 3rd, 4th, 5th, 6th, 7th, 8th, 9th, 10th, 11th, 12th, 13th, 14th, 15th, 16th, 17th, and 18th Regiments of Irregular Cavalry, the same.

CHAPTER V

1857-1859

THE INDIAN MUTINY—MULTAN—DEFENCE OF CHICHAWATNI

EARLY in May when the news of the outbreaks at Meerut and Delhi reached Multan, the native officers brought to Major Chamberlain's notice the fact that there was considerable disaffection in the two Native Infantry Regiments, the 62nd and the 69th, then in the station. The Woordi Major Risaldar Mir Barkat Ali and Risaldar Mir Banda Ali were specially useful to him at this juncture, but it is not too much to say that the whole Regiment was loyal to the core. The men were approached by sepoys of the 62nd and 69th N.I., who attempted to tamper with their loyalty, and by threats as well as by bribes, to induce them to throw their lot in with theirs, and rise against the British. The sowars not only refused their offers, but also told the intending rebels they would act against them at once if they mutinied, and threatened to make prisoners of them if they repeated their attempts to seduce them from their duty. The men duly recounted everything to their native officers, who repeated what they heard to Major Chamberlain. All this was unknown to the officers of the disaffected Regiments, and indeed to all but those to whom Major Chamberlain had reported it. But for the information given by the native officers to Major Chamberlain, it would probably have remained unknown till too late. Major Chamberlain had kept the Officer Commanding at Multan, Colonel Hicks, informed and by him was ordered to assemble the native officers of all Corps in Garrison, and inquire from them if disaffection existed in their respective Regiments. The Subadar Major of the 69th N.I. professed his entire ignorance of the existence of any disaffection, whereupon Mir Barkat Ali rose and reproached him for his falsehoods, and eventually compelled him to admit that a mutinous feeling did exist.

At midnight of the 9th/10th June, orders were received for a general parade of all the troops at 6 a.m. next morning. The men of the 62nd N.I., and the 69th N.I., were ordered to lay down their arms. The former complied in a cheerful and soldierly manner, but the men of the 69th were sullen and discontented and inclined to refuse, till the Cavalry, wheeling outwards, formed on their flanks and disclosed a battery of guns directed on them with port fires alight. The sepoys then gave in, the few who refused being forcibly disarmed. The native officers were allowed to retain their swords, and it was explained to the men that they had nothing to fear as long as they remained quiet, but that any rioters or deserters would be severely dealt with. The arms and ammunition were lodged in the Fort and Cavalry patrolled the Station till all fear of trouble was at an end.

The following facts should be borne in mind. There were no British troops in the garrison, and the behaviour of the 1st Irregular Cavalry and of the Artillery had saved Multan and relieved Government of all apprehension in this quarter. Major Chamberlain, though not the senior officer in the station, had been specially selected by Sir John Lawrence, the Governor-General, to carry out the operation. The Governor-General and others expressed their warm thanks to Major Chamberlain and the 1st Irregular Cavalry for this proof of their loyalty and devotion to the Government. Special notice was taken of the services rendered by Woordi Major Mir Barkat Ali, who received a reward in money and a Khilat, as also did Risaldars Karamat Ali and Mir Bandey Ali. The

Subadar of the 69th N.I., together with several men of that Regiment, were tried by Court Martial and executed.

During this time a large number of the men of the Regiment were at home on furlough. Several rejoined the Regiment at the outbreak of the mutiny, others were collected by Risaldar Ghulam Ali, and marched with him to place themselves under the orders of the Officer Commanding the nearest body of troops. Risaldar Mir Bisharat Ali did the same elsewhere, and there were not more than two or three men on furlough who did not similarly prove their loyalty.

In September the nomadic tribes in the Gogaira District rose in revolt, and Major Chamberlain was ordered to move with 150 sabres of his Regiment towards the Ravi where a large body of rebels was collected. On reaching Chichawatni, on the 23rd September, he was attacked by several thousands of the rebels, both mounted and on foot, and was compelled—like Skinner before him—to seize and occupy a fortified serai, where he would be able to hold the enemy at bay till he was relieved. The serai had the village on the one side and on the other three sides had a thick jungle, with high grass close up to the walls. The serai was not occupied without a skirmish in which the Detachment sustained a loss of eight killed and wounded and killed about thirty of the enemy. There was a little fodder in the serai, and some grain was seized in the village ; a stream about fifty yards from the walls supplied water. The supply, however, was insufficient, there was no Medical Officer, and no medical stores or medicines for the wounded. There were only two camel loads of ammunition, and Major Chamberlain wrote to Multan asking for assistance, and for Artillery and ammunition, with which he felt he could carry out the necessary operations in the district. He said his only apprehension was the difficulty of restraining the over-keenness of his men. The defences of the serai were strengthened, the gate barricaded, and the summit of the walls and roofs of the towers protected by a parapet made of saddles, baggage, and whatever else was available.

Next morning the enemy made a half-hearted attack but were beaten off without difficulty, losing a few killed and wounded.

The attack was repeated later with greater energy, and a heavy fire was poured upon the serai, but owing to the measures for providing cover, the Detachment had only two men killed and five wounded, while about fourteen of the enemy were killed. The horses were mostly loose, and without rations, and officers and men had nothing to eat but boiled gram. All the grass-cutters were armed with lathis and held in readiness to defend the serai, if the enemy attempted to carry it by storm.

An attempt was made to collect bhoosa and grass for the horses, but in this ten men were cut off by the enemy and killed. The rebels tried to induce the native officers and men to give up the British Officers (there were two civil officers with Major Chamberlain), offering among other things to make Woordi Major Mir Barkat Ali Nawab of Multan, but the only answer they got was that " the path to the capture of their officers lay over the bodies of the whole Detachment."

In this way the little siege continued, the horses practically without food, the officers and men on the smallest ration of gram, frequently under heavy fire both by day and night.

After four days' investment, a relieving force arrived from Multan, having marched twenty-five miles a day. Relieved and relievers remained at Chichawatni three days more, during which time the serai was properly fortified, provisioned and garrisoned. The General wrote to thank Major Chamberlain and those under him for the gallant defence they had made under trying circumstances. The following received special promotion for their conduct while besieged ; Kot-Dafadar Khawani Khan and Zabteh

Khan to Naib Ressaidars, Sowar Imam Ali Khan to Dafadar.

At the beginning of October, Major Chamberlain was, by the Governor-General's orders, placed in command of a column to act against a large force of rebels on the west bank of the Ravi. On the approach of the column the rebels took refuge in some large jungles near Jullee, the extraordinary thickness of which rendered it impossible for mounted troops to get at them. Every possible attempt was made to drive them into the open, and to set the jungle on fire for this purpose, but it was unsuccessful, and it was only after the lapse of twelve days, when a column with infantry and guns moved up the east bank of the river, that the rebels made off, and having misled the mounted troops by false information, practically evaded all pursuit.

Some infantry joined Major Chamberlain's column, and he kept open the communications between Multan and Lahore, till the Regiment returned to the latter at the end of November. It remained there till April 1858, when it moved in relief to Jullunder.

For their gallant and loyal conduct throughout the serious days of the mutiny and for conspicuous bravery in action, the following were specially brought to notice and rewarded by Government :

Ressaidar and Woordi Major Mir Barkat Ali, a large grant of land, 1st Class Order of British India, and promotion to Risaldar.

Ressaidar Elahi Bukhsh Khan, Order of British India, 2nd Class.

Ressaidar Ikhtyar Khan, Order of British India, 2nd Class.

Ressaidar Shaikh Ghulam Nabi, Order of British India, 2nd Class.

Naib Ressaidar Shydad Khan, Order of British India, 2nd Class.

Naib Ressaidar Sheikh Kutub-un-din, **Order of British
    India, 2nd Class.**
Naib Ressaidar Mirza Shadi Beg, **Order of Merit.**
Jemadar Hukum Singh, **Order of Merit.**
Dafadar Sadik Ali, **Order of Merit.**
Dafadar Saadat Ali, **Order of Merit,**

while other non-commissioned officers and men received
rewards testifying that their loyal services to Government
had not been overlooked.

The village on the land granted to Mir Barkat Ali was
called " Barkatabab," to commemorate the name of Mir
Barkat Ali.   It is situated at a little distance from Khar-
kauda, the native town of the Sardar Bahadur.   The
land, with an income of about Rs.12,000 annually, is now
in possession of his heirs.

Ressaidar Elahi Bukhsh Khan was a Pathan of Jhajar,
District Bulandshahar.   He received twenty-two wounds
in a fight at Chichawatni, but lived long after to enjoy
the rewards of his bravery and loyalty.

Ressaidar Shydad Khan was a Rajput of Kanhur,
District Rohtak.   His father, Jemadar Zamurdi Khan,
was one of the oldest soldiers enlisted by Captain Skinner
in the Regiment.   Shydad Khan served most loyally
and gallantly for forty-eight years with the Regiment,
and received the 1st Class Order of British India, before
he retired.   Several members of his family have since
served with the Regiment, such as Risaldar Major Abdul
Ghafur Khan, Bahadur (his nephew), and the late Ressaidar
Ibrahim Khan (his eldest son).   Two of his grandsons,
Risaldar Mohammed Ilyas Khan and Ressaidar Khuda
Bukhsh Khan, and one of his great-grandsons, Sowar
Mohammed Ayub Khan, were serving in the Regiment in
1908.

Ressaidar Shekh Kutbuddin was a resident of Hasan-
garh, near Kharkhauda.   He was Woordi Major for a
long time and finally Risaldar Major before he retired.

Extract from the Bengal Army List " January 1863 "

BENGAL CAVALRY

1st BENGAL CAVALRY (LATE 1st IRREGULAR CAVALRY)

Detachment : " Bhurtpore." " Candhar, 1842."
Headquarters at Meerut. Detachment at Delhi.

Rank, Names, and Corps.	Army Rank.	Appointment.	Remarks.
Colonel C. T. Chamberlain, Staff Corps	14 April 1862	19 Nov. 1849	Commandant.
Lieutenant G. C. Thomson, Staff Corps.	7 Sept. 1854	20 July 1858	Second in Command.
Lieutenant A. R. Chapman, Staff Corps.	24 Sept. 1857	2 April 1863	Adjutant.
Lieutenant A. W. C. Read, 51st Foot P.H.	17 Nov. 1857	—	—
Captain D. Compton, late 2nd E.L.C.	6 Dec. 1857	22 Mar. 1862	Commanding Detachment at Delhi.
Lieutenant A. Lindsay, late 68th N.I. P.H.	18 May 1858	12 June 1861	Paid doing duty Officer. With 7th Dn. Gds. as a temporary measure.
Lieutenant H. C. Creak, late 4th E.L.C.	2 Jan. 1860	5 Feb. 1862	Lv. to the Presidency to study the native languages, to 20th Sept.
Lieutenant D. G. A. Jackson, Genl. List, Cavalry. P.H.	1 Jan. 1862	23 Feb. 1863	Paid doing duty Officer.
Assistant Surgeon C. Prentis .	27 Jan. 1858	—	In temp. Med. Charge
Ressaldar Meer Burkut Alee	—	1 Aug. 1857	Sirdar Bahadoor.
Ressaldar Bahadoor Ally .	—	—	Sirdar Bahadoor.
Ressaldar Shydad Khan.	—	20 Oct. 1858	Bahadoor.
Woordie Major Shaikh Kootub Oodeen	—	29 Oct. 1858	Bahadoor.

Establishment : 6 Troops, 3 Ressaldars, 3 Ressaidars, 1 Woordie Major, 6 Jemadars, 6 Kote Duffadars, 48 Duffadars, 6 Nishanburdars, 6 Trumpeters, 384 Sowars.

CHAPTER VI

1859–1896

In February 1859 a wing of the Regiment was ordered to move rapidly to Ferozepore to take part in operations against a large band of rebels in the neighbourhood of Sirsa, and was employed on this duty for two months, when it returned to Jullunder. The rebels showed but little fight, and dispersed into small parties as the troops approached.

In 1861 the designation of the Regiment was changed to the 1st " Bengal Cavalry."

The Regiment moved in relief to Delhi and Meerut in 1862.

The numbers of all ranks in the Bengal Cavalry had been twice reduced, and now stood at 384, the lowest it had ever been.

In 1864 the Regiment was sent in course of relief to Nowgong, furnishing detachments to Jubblepore and Nagode.

Colonel Crawford Chamberlain was promoted General in 1867, and vacated command of the Regiment. He was succeeded by Major W. R. E. Alexander.

General Chamberlain later commanded the Lucknow Division. He retired in 1872, was appointed K.C.B., in 1897, and died in 1903.

In 1867 the Regiment relieved the 16th Cavalry at Marar.

The Regiment in 1871 moved in relief to Cawnpore, taking part in the large camp of exercise at Delhi en route.

1872.—This year Risaldar Major Mir Barkat Ali died from the effects of a fall from his horse—" a brave soldier and a staunch supporter of the Government and a friend of all ranks," as the Regimental Order announcing his death described him.

Woordi Major Sheikh Kutubdin received the 1st Class and Risaldar James Hawes the 2nd Class of the Order of British India with effect from 1868.

Risaldar Major Sheikh Bahadur Ali was of Sohna, District Gurgaon. He had been transferred from the old 9th Cavalry. Several members of his family have served in the Regiment, viz. Risaldar Major Sheikh Abdul Kadar Khan Bahadur (his cousin), and Risaldar Kutab Khan (his son-in-law). Another son-in-law, and younger brother of Risaldar Kutab Khan, is Muhammad Syeed Khan, who was Risaldar Major of the Regiment in 1907. Jemadar Sheikh Abdul Majid, who was serving with the Regiment in 1908, is one of the grandsons of Sheikh Bahadur Ali.

In 1876 the Regiment moved to Sialkot. Risaldar Major Sheikh Bahadur Ali, a gallant soldier and a faithful servant to Goverment, whose loss was deeply mourned, died this year.

Colonel R. Jenkins succeeded Colonel Alexander in command of the Regiment.

In February 1879 the Regiment was ordered to Kohat on service and occupied the outposts on the Baru and Thull roads. Cholera broke out but was soon stamped out, and the Headquarters were moved to Thull. The posts between Thull and Kurram were held by detachments of the Regiment who were employed on convoy duties and in keeping open the communications between those places as well as between Thull and Hangu. Frequent attacks and raids were made on this line. A Detachment under Jemadar (late Risaldar Major) Gulam Mustapha Khan accompanied Sir F. Roberts in his advance over the Shutergardun and on to Kabul, where it remained till the end of the War. Another Detachment accompanied Major-General Tytler on the Zaimukht expedition, and gained the commendation of the General for the way it had carried out its duties.

In April 1880 one of the outposts—at Chapri—under Lieutenant W. H. Cazalet, was attacked by some 2,000

Extract from the Bengal Army List " July 1879 "

1st BENGAL CAVALRY (LATE 1st IRREGULAR CAVALRY)

"Bhurtpore." Detachment: "Candhar, 1842."

SIALKOT.—Arrived 1st February 1876 from Cawnpore.   At Kohat on Field Service.   Under orders to Nowshera.

Date of First Commission.	Rank, Names, and Corps.	Army Rank.	First Appointment to Regiment.	Present Appointment in Regiment.	Remarks.
	COMMANDANT.				
20 Feb. 1845	Colonel R. Jenkins, Bengal Cavalry P.H.	20 Feb. 1876	2 Jan. 1868	1 April 187	Fur., m. c., 2 years 23 March 1878.
	SQUADRON COMMANDERS.				
19 July 1851	Lieutenant-Colonel G. C. Thomson, S. C. P.H.	19 July 1877	20 July 1858	8 Mar. 1879	Officiating Commandant.
4 Jan. 1856	Major A. R. Chapman, S.C. . P.H.	4 Jan. 1876	2 Apl. 1863	8 Mar. 1879	Officiating Second in Command.
11 Aug. 1857	Major T. M. B. Glascock, S.C. . P.H.	11 Aug. 1877	8 Aug. 1876	1 Mar. 1878	Dharmsala, m., c., [6 mos.
	SQUADRON OFFICERS.				
11 July 1865	Captain F. C. Burton, p.s., S.C. . H.S.	11 July 1877	1 May 1869	1 Mar. 1878	Punjab Chiefs' Contingent.
4 Feb. 1861	Captain W. A. Lawrence, S.C. . P.H.	4 Feb. 1873	20 Mar. 1873	20 Mar. 1873	On Field Transport Service.
	MEDICAL OFFICERS.				
20 Oct. 1853	Surgeon-Major A. J. Dale, M.B. Attached.	20 Oct. 1873	1 Mar. 1877	1 Mar. 1877	—
27 Mar. 1872	Lieutenant G. B. Renny, S.C. H.S.	27 Mar. 1872	23 May 1876	1 Mar. 1879	Officiating Adjutant.
11 Sept. 1873	Lieutenant A. Mac W. Rennay, R. Art. (S.C. pro.)	11 Sept. 1873	24 Jan. 1878	1 May 1879	Officiating Squadron Officer.
22 Sept. 1876	Honorary Lieutenant Alexander Van Cortlandt Skinner .	22 Sept. 1876	—	—	—

Date of entering Service.	Native Officers.	Date of Commissions as			Remarks.
		Jemadar.	Ressaidar.	Ressaldar.	
	RESSALDARS.				
1 Mar. 1844	Mirza Ewaz Beg .	17 Apl. 1857	9 June 1872	12 Oct. 1873	Ressaldar Major, 19 Oct. 1876.
22 Nov. 1851	Mohammad Ubdool Kadur .	9 June 1873	12 Oct. 1876	19 Oct. 1876	—
15 Sept. 1859	Jowahar Singh .	12 Oct. 1873	19 Oct. 1876	17 Oct. 1878	—
	RESSAIDARS.				
4 Oct. 1851	Ukbur Ullee .	14 Sept. 1873	7 Dec. 1876	—	Woordie Major.
1 May 1853	Nujeeb Beg .	1 May 1875	1 Apl. 1878	—	—
15 Feb. 1844	Wullee Mohamed Khan .	16 Oct. 1875	1 May 1878	—	—
1 May 1851	Soorajoodeen .	7 Dec. 1876	17 Oct. 1878	—	—
	JAMADARS.				
30 Nov. 1848	Kurrum Khan .	19 Oct. 1876	—	—	—
10 July 1843	Meer Umeer Ullee .	1 May 1877	—	—	—
28 Dec. 1854	Gholam Fareed Khan .	1 Apl. 1878	—	—	—
15 Nov. 1867	Kootub Khan .	1 May 1878	—	—	—
6 Nov. 1854	Raheem Buksh Khan .	1 Oct. 1878	—	—	—
1 May 1856	Gholam Moostuffa Khan .	17 Oct. 1878	—	—	—

Uniform: Yellow. Facings: Black. Lace: Gold. Armament: Snider Carbines.

Each Regiment of Bengal Cavalry consists of 6 Troops with the following Establishment: Commandant, 3 Squadron Commanders, 3 Squadron Officers, 1 Medical Officer, 3 Ressaidars, 1 Woordie Major, 6 Jemadars, 6 Kote Duffadars, 48 Duffadars (including 1 Farrier Major and 1 Salootrie), 6 Trumpeters, 384 Sowars (including 1 Assistant Salootrie and 6 Farriers). See G.G.O. No. 494, 31 May 1861, and Government letter No. 677, 31 January 1863; G.G.O. No. 1092, 20 October 1873.

Regulations for the Dress and Equipment of the Bengal Cavalry, see G.O. No. 29 of 1874 and G.O. 43 of 1875. Temporarily augmented to a strength of 480 sowars; G.G.O. No. 1A, dated 7 December 1878.

Waziris.   The defences of the post were of the most trifling description, and some of the enemy got inside the post, but were killed and the rest driven off, our loss being only one killed, Sowar Yakub Khan of Jhajjar, Rohtak District, and several wounded.

In September Colonel R. Jenkins died of fever. He was succeeded in the command by Major A. R. Chapman.

In November the Regiment concentrated at Kohat, and the War coming to an end, marched to Cawnpore.

Its losses during the War were, killed or died of disease : 2 British officers, 4 native officers, 8 non-commissioned officers, 51 sowars.

Sowar Mazhar Ali Khan, while acting as orderly to Major-General Sir F. Roberts, at Kila Kazi, on the 11th December 1879, saw one of the enemy taking aim at the General, from behind a bank at about 40 yards distance. Mazhar Ali rode at him, his horse was shot, but Mazhar Ali threw himself on the man in a deep ditch of water, seized him by the throat and held him till another orderly came up and speared him.   For this act of gallantry Mazhar Ali Khan was promoted to Dafadar, and in 1887 received the Order of Merit.   Mazhar Ali Khan rose to be a Ressaidar in the Regiment and received the 2nd Class Order of British India, previous to his retirement on pension in 1903.

The Regiment in 1884 marched from Cawnpore to Peshawar, and soon after its arrival marched to Landi Kotal to form the escort for His Highness Abdur Rahman Khan, Amir of Afghanistan, who was visiting India, and on his return in April, it again escorted him to the Frontier near Landi Kotal.

In September 1887 Colonel Chapman completed his tenure of command, and was succeeded by Colonel R. Morris.

In November Risaldar Major Ghulam Mustapha Khan received the 2nd Class Order of British India.   The decoration was presented to him by the Commander-in-Chief,

Sir F. Roberts, at a parade of all the troops in Garrison. Sir F. Roberts also presented the Order of Merit to Kot Dafadar Mazhar Ali Khan, who had earned it as mentioned above in 1879. His Excellency the Viceroy, Lord Dufferin, was also present ; the Regiment furnished numerous escorts for His Excellency during his stay in Peshawar.

This year an Inspector-General of Cavalry was appointed for the first time, and General Luck, who was appointed to the post, inspected the Regiment in March 1888.

In November 1888 the Regiment left Peshawar, and after taking part in a camp of exercise at Rawal Pindi, marched to Saugor, and furnished Detachments to Jubblepore and Sutna.

1893.—Dafadar (later Risaldar) Ismail Khan was selected to form part of the escort of Native Cavalry sent to England on the occasion of the opening of the Imperial Institute by Her Majesty the Queen Empress. Dafadar Ismail Khan was promoted Jemadar by order of the Government on his return.

In this year a squadron of Punjabi Mohammedans from the Ludhiana and Ferozepore Districts was raised. Jemadar Muhammad Kashamsham was transferred to the Regiment from the 10th Lancers.

Muhammad Kashamsham was of the Sadozai family, descendants of Shah Shuja, Amir of Afghanistan, and resided at Ludhiana. He served as Woordi Major, and Risaldar, and died at Lucknow in 1908.

In the year 1894 Colonel Morris vacated command of the Regiment, and was succeeded by Major R. F. Gartside Tipping.

In November the Regiment marched to Meerut, where it was stationed till 1898.

The Regiment was converted into a Lancer Regiment in 1896, and its designation now was the " 1st Bengal Lancers." The red loongi and kummerband were abolished, and replaced by black ones.

Extract from the Bengal Army List "July 1897"

1ST REGIMENT OF BENGAL LANCERS, LATE 1ST IRREGULAR CAVALRY (SKINNER'S HORSE)

(Raised in 1803).

Class Regiment—4 Squadrons Hindustani Mahomedans.
"Bhurtpore",—"Candhar, 1842",—"Afghanistan, 1879–80."
Uniform: Yellow. Facings: Black.

MEERUT.—Arrived, 17 December 1894, from Suegor. Detachment at Delhi.

First Commission.	Rank, Name, and Corps.	Army Rank.	First Appointment to Regiment.	Present Appointment in Regiment.	Remarks.
	COMMANDANT.				
3 Aug. 1873	Major (Temporary Lieutenant-Colonel) Gartside-Tipping, R.F. (p.s.).	3 Aug. 1893	20 July 1879	10 Sept. 1894	—
	SQUADRON COMMANDERS.				
1 Dec. 1869	Colonel St. F. F. Mitchell, (p.s.)	26 Mar. 1895	1 July 1882	18 Sept.1885	Second in Command, 20 Feb., 1893. Assistant Q.M.G. Punjab Command. Leave out of India, p.a., 1 year, P.C.O., 11 Apl. 1896; Extension. p.a. 1 year.
1 Oct. 1874	Major C. H. Hayes (p.s.)	1 Oct. 1894	18 July 1883	6 May 1887	Second in Command, 10 Sept. 1894.
1 May 1878	Captain W. D. Thomson (p.s.)	1 May 1889	13 Sept.1880	22 Feb. 1888	Judge-Advocate-General's Department.
23 Apl. 1881	Captain H. L. Roberts (p.s.)	25 Aug. 1894	27 Oct. 1885	30 Oct. 1894	Officiating D.A.A.G. (District Staff, Bengal Command).
25 Aug. 1883	Captain C. Davis (p.s.)	23 Apl. 1892	21 May 1885	4 Aug. 1891	Leave out of India, p.a., 8 months, 9 July 1896; Extension till 8 Sept. 1897.
	SQUADRON OFFICERS.				
30 Jan. 1884	Captain C. Finch (p.s.)	30 Jan. 1895	8 Sept. 1887	22 Feb. 1888	—
7 Feb. 1885	Captain C. P. G. Griffin (p.s.)	7 Feb. 1896	26 Apl. 1890	26 Apl. 1890	—
5 Feb. 1887	Lieutenant H. M. Grove	1 Nov. 1888	21 Dec. 1889	10 Sept. 1894	Russia, on duty.
21 Sept.1889	Lieutenant C. A. K. Johnson	15 Sept.1891	6 Aug. 1892	3 Aug. 1895	Adjutant, 3 Aug. 1895. Leave out of India, m.c., 1 year, 12 May 1896; Extension, m.c., 4 months.

Date of entering Service	Names				Remarks
	MEDICAL OFFICER.				
31 Mar. 1888	Surgeon-Captain G. T. Mould	31 Mar. 1888	20 Aug. 1890	4 Aug. 1892	—
	ATTACHED.				
23 Oct. 1889	Lieutenant C. L. Gaussen	5 Aug. 1891	3 Mar. 1895	3 Mar. 1895	Officiating Squadron Officer. Leave out of India, m.c., 1 year, 5 Mar.
29 Nov. 1890	Lieutenant A. S. H. Teed, (W.g. Officer, 17 B.I.)	13 Sept.1892	12 Oct. 1896	12 Oct. 1896	Officiating Squadron Officer. [1897.
30 Aug. 1893	Lieutenant F. D. Russell	30 Nov. 1895	25 Nov. 1895	25 Nov. 1895	Officiating Adjutant.
20 Feb. 1893	Honorary Lieutenant S. E. Skinner	10 Feb. 1893	10 Feb. 1893	10 Feb. 1893	Not attached for duty.

NATIVE OFFICERS.

Date of entering Service.	Names.	Jemadar.	Ressaidar.	Risaldar.	Risaldar Major.	Remarks.
	RISALDAR MAJOR.					
1 Jan. 1868	Abdul Ghafur Khan	23 Sept.1879	20 Oct. 1879	13 Dec. 1883	1 Mar. 1890	—
	RISALDARS.					
24 Mar. 1868	Mir Afzal Ali	22 Nov. 1879	23 May 1883	18 Sept.1885	—	—
6 Apl. 1872	Wazir Ali Khan	1 May 1882	1 May 1885	1 Mar. 1890	—	—
1 May 1872	Sher Khan (14)	23 May 1883	14 Dec. 1886	16 May 1896	—	—
	RESSAIDARS.					
8 Oct. 1881	Muzaffar Ali (14)	21 Nov. 1883	1 May 1889	—	—	—
1 Feb. 1872	Abdullah Khan	18 Sept.1885	1 Mar. 1890	—	—	—
1 Feb. 1877	Muhammad Sayyid Khan	1 Oct. 1885	1 May 1891	—	—	—
1 Feb. 1868	Umdeh Khan	23 Feb. 1887	23 Oct. 1894	—	—	—
29 Dec. 1885	Muhammad Kasham Sham	1 Nov. 1893	16 May 1896	—	—	—
	JEMADARS.					
1 May 1869	Mazhar Ali Khan	1 May 1889	—	—	—	—
1 May 1866	Sipahdar Khan	1 Mar. 1890	—	—	—	Woordie Major, 16 May 1896.
5 May 1869	Salih Muhammad Khan	16 Mar. 1890	—	—	—	—
1 May 1870	Abdullah Khan	16 Feb. 1891	—	—	—	Order of Merit, third [class.
10 Sept.1871	Abdulkarim Khan	1 May 1891	—	—	—	—
5 July 1881	Ismail Khan (14)	6 July 1893	—	—	—	—
31 May 1874	Suleman Khan	23 Oct. 1894	—	—	—	—
1 Nov. 1885	Muhammad Ilyas Khan	16 May 1896	—	—	—	—

CHAPTER VII

1897–1901

THE CHINA EXPEDITION—RELIEF OF PEKIN

In 1897 details of the Regiment proceeded to Kohat with transport and took part in the Tirah Expedition, and subsequently in that against the Boxers.

Captain C. Davis, Captain C. G. P. Griffen, and Lieutenant F. D. Russell served in these campaigns.

The Regiment marched to Lucknow in the spring of 1898. On the 2nd December it was warned for service, and ordered to join the Malakand Field Force, assembling at Malakand. The Regiment was ready to start on the 5th when orders were received to stand fast, and a week later, as it appeared that in all probability there would be no necessity for an expedition, the Regiment was directed to proceed by double marches to Aligarh to join the 2nd Division of Cavalry at a Camp of Exercise at Delhi. The Regiment returned to Lucknow in February, when it was ordered to demobilise.

In 1899 His Royal Highness the Duke of York was appointed Honorary Colonel of the Regiment, which was now designated the 1st (Duke of York's Own) Bengal Lancers.

His Royal Highness presented a silver cup, for which a competition between squadrons takes place annually.

He was graciously pleased to accept an address from the Indian ranks of the Regiment, in which they testified to the loyalty and devotion of all ranks to Her Majesty the Queen and to the Royal Family, and expressed their gratification for the honour done to the Corps by His Royal Highness's appointment.

In 1900 a small party was sent with horses for Mounted Infantry to South Africa, and remained there on duty throughout the campaign.   Captain C. Davis and Lieutenant F. D. Russell also served in South Africa, but rejoined the unit in China.

On the 19th June orders were received for the Regiment to prepare for active service in China, and all was soon ready.   But as no transports were ready the Regiment did not leave Lucknow till the 1st July and railed to Calcutta.

His Royal Highness the Duke of York telegraphed to congratulate the Regiment on being selected for service on this expedition.   At Calcutta the Regiment embarked on three transports and after a rather bad passage, owing to the monsoon in the Bay of Bengal, reached Hongkong, and went on to Taku, where the Force disembarked.   The Regiment was railed to Tientsin and reached there on the 2nd August, and joined the force under the command of Sir. A. Gaselee, K.C.B.   The American, Japanese, French, German, and Russian Forces were also collecting there for the relief of the Legations in Pekin, which were besieged by the Boxers.   Owing to the energy of the Commander of the British, who announced his intention of moving at once, while some other Commanders wished to await further reinforcements, the allied forces began the advance on Pekin on the 4th August.   The Regiment left a small detachment at Tientsin.

On the 5th August the Chinese position at Peitsang on the Peiho was attacked, the Regiment covering the left flank of the British during the advance, and joining later with the Japanese Cavalry in operating against the enemy's right.   The country was difficult for cavalry owing to the crops, which were often higher than a mounted man's head.   The Chinese did not wait for the cavalry attack, but several stragglers were captured in the high crops, also a field gun, which is now in the Officers' Mess, taken by a Patrol of " B " Squadron under Dafadar Saif Khan.

Two Squadrons were sent to reconnoitre ahead and the Chinese retired across the Peiho.

The casualties in the Regiment this day were Risaldar Sher Khan and Ressaidar Mazhar Ali Khan and one Sowar, Ali Nur Kahn (Pathan of Lohari), wounded and two horses killed.

Next day the allied forces advanced to Yangtsun, where the enemy held a strong position, which the allies attacked and after some resistance compelled the enemy to evacuate. The Regiment this day covered the right flank. The thick and high crops prevented any effectual pursuit when the enemy retired from his position. The advance continued, and on the 9th August two Squadrons, under Major C. H. Hayes, charged a large body of the enemy, dispersing his infantry, and cutting up forty or fifty of the Tartar Cavalry and capturing three standards, taken by a Troop of " B " Squadron under Ressaidar Mohamed Ilyas Khan, while our casualties amounted to only a few men wounded and two horses killed.

The heat all the time of the advance was very great, some horses died and several men were incapacitated by sunstroke.

On the 11th August some barges were observed on the far side of the Peiho, which the enemy were busily engaged in unloading. Lance-Dafadar Imam Ali Khan swam across the river and secured the barges, which it was found contained gunpowder, and they were brought over to our side. For this he received the Order of Merit.

On the 14th August the allied forces assaulted and carried the walls of Pekin ; the Russians, Americans, and Japanese who attacked the East Gate suffered heavy loss ; the British Column met with little resistance at first and passed through the Chinese City without trouble, but was met with heavy fire from the wall of the Tartar City as it approached the South Gate. The gate was breached and twenty volunteers of the 1st Lancers (including three native officers, namely, Risaldar (afterwards Risaldar

Major) Wazir Ali Khan, Ressaidar (later Risaldar) Ismail Khan and Jemadar Amir Ali Khan), under Lieutenant Macaulay, with some fifty men from Native Infantry Regiments, rushed the breach, and drove the enemy from the walls, inflicting heavy loss on him in so doing.

A party from the British Force, discovering an unguarded water gate, reached the Legations before all other troops and while fighting was still going on.

The next few days were spent in completing the conquest of the city, the 1st Bengal Lancers patrolling the Chinese City and protecting it from the depredations of Chinese and others.

On the 19th August a large number of Boxers collected in the Imperial Hunting Park. A column consisting of 1st Lancers, two guns and a Battalion of Native Infantry, the whole under Lieutenant-Colonel Gartside Tipping, was sent out to deal with them. A patrol under Risaldar Wazir Ali Khan was surrounded and attacked, but assisted by Lieutenant Macaulay, Woordi Major Mohamed Kasham Sham and Dafadar Habibur Rahman Khan pluckily beat off the attack, Lance-Dafadar Karimudin and the rest of the patrol distinguishing themselves. The Infantry and guns came into action and dispersed the enemy with some loss.

Lord Roberts, Commander-in-Chief in South Africa, telegraphed from Pretoria to convey his congratulations on the successful charge made by the Regiment on the 9th of August. The Government intimated its approval of the skill, courage, and endurance of the troops during the advance and at the occupation of Pekin.

A telegram of congratulation and of sympathy with the wounded from Her Majesty The Queen Empress was also received.

On the 27th August, detachments from all units participated in a triumphal march through the Forbidden City.

Though organised resistance was at an end, small

expeditions were necessary to disperse bodies of Boxers and inflict punishments for atrocities commited earlier on European missionaries and others, and some incidents in connection with these expeditions call for notice.

In September Captain C. P. G. Griffin with half a squadron accompanied a German force against the walled town of Liang Hasiang, some twenty miles south of Pekin. Captain Griffin found himself with about sixteen men, the rest being out on patrol and on other duties, face to face with a large body of Boxers, whom he at once charged and dispersed. His horse, however, was shot under him, and he would have been killed but for the gallantry of Trumpeter Ali Sher Khan, who stood over him and shot two of the enemy with his revolver. Ali Sher Khan was awarded for his conduct with the Order of Merit.

In the same month Captain Browne of the Central India Horse, who was attached to the Regiment during the expedition, with twenty men attacked a considerable number of Boxers, who had surrounded an American foraging party. Captain Browne drove them into a village, into which he followed, and driving them out into the open, inflicted heavy loss on them and dispersed them.

At Tientsin, Lieutenant Gaussen of the 2nd Corps, also attached to the Regiment during the expedition, with twenty-five men of the 1st Bengal Lancers and a party of American Cavalry charged a force of Boxers and inflicted severe loss on them, Lieutenant Gaussen saving the life of an American officer, who was on the point of falling into the hands of the enemy. Lance-Dafadar Abdur Raham (of Sohna) was severely wounded and had to be invalided.

For this act of gallantry, Lieutenant Gaussen was rewarded with the D.S.O.

Active operations had practically come to an end, when in November three Squadrons sailed to Hongkong, where they remained till May 1901.

In 1901 "A" Squadron remained on duty in North China

between Tientsin and Fengtai, busily engaged in checking the depredation of robber bands.

The cold throughout the winter was most intense, but there was no sickness, and no deaths but that of Sowar Abdus Sammand Khan, killed in action.

In the summer the Regiment was ordered back to India and reached Lucknow in July. The following rewards were given for work during the expedition, besides those already mentioned :

Lieutenant-Colonel Gartside Tipping, C.B.

Captain Griffin ⎫
Lieutenant Gaussen ⎭ Distinguished Service Order.

Risaldar Major Abdul Ghafur Khan ⎫ Order of British
Risaldar Sher Khan ⎭ India, 2nd Class.

On the 10th September, Lieutenant-Colonel Gartside Tipping vacated the command, and was succeeded by Lieutenant-Colonel C. H. Hayes.

Extracts from Indian Army List "July 1914"

1ST DUKE OF YORK'S OWN LANCERS (SKINNER'S HORSE)

PESHAWAR.—Arrived, 28th March 1912, from Dera Ismail Khan.

"Bhurtpore" "Candahar, 1842" "Afghanistan, 1879–80" "Pekin, 1900."

Composition—4 Squadrons of Hindustani Musalmans.   Uniform—Yellow Facings—Black velvet.

Colonel-in-Chief.—The King.

Honorary Colonel.—Major-General His Highness Sir Madho Rao Scindia, Bahadur, Maharaja of Gwalior, G.C.S.I., G.C.V.O., A.D.C.   1st January 1906.

First Commission or Date of Entering Service.	Names and Rank.	Army Rank.	Present Appointment in Regiment.	Remarks.
	COMMANDANT.			
12 Nov. 1884	Lieutenant-Colonel C. Bailey	12 Nov. 1910	1 Apl. 1912	—
	SQUADRON COMMANDERS (4).			
16 Nov. 1887	Lieutenant-Colonel P. Holland-Pryor, M.V.O. (Q)	16 Nov. 1913	1 Apl. 1912	Second in Command.
30 Aug. 1893	Major F. D. Russell, p.s.c., L. (Q)	30 Aug. 1911	30 June 1906	—
10 Oct. 1894	Major D. I. M. Macaulay, L (Q)	10 Oct. 1912	1 July 1906	—
28 Sept. 1895	Captain E. G. Sexton	28 Sept. 1904	1 Apl. 1912	—
	SQUADRON OFFICERS (9).			
5 Aug. 1896	Captain H. B. Cheyne	5 Aug. 1905	1 Apl. 1900	—
16 Feb. 1898	Captain A. F. M. Binny	16 Feb. 1907	5 Oct. 1901	—
20 Jan. 1900	Captain R. B. C. Raban	20 Jan. 1909	17 Feb. 1903	—
27 Jan. 1900	Captain A. Chamberlayne	2 Mar. 1909	18 Jan. 1903	—
18 July 1900	Captain J. A. Muirhead, p.s.c.	18 July 1909	9 Apl. 1902	—
8 Jan. 1901	Captain E. H. Pott	8 Jan. 1910	24 Nov. 1905	—
22 July 1903	Captain H. Gillies	12 Dec. 1911	11 Mar. 1906	—
22 July 1903	Captain G. A. C. Wetherall	22 July 1912	29 Sept. 1906	Adjutant.
5 Aug. 1905	Lieutenant A. A. M. Beaman	5 Nov. 1905	1 Apl. 1907	Adjutant.
29 Jan. 1910	Lieutenant D. M. V. Veitch	29 Apl. 1912	6 Mar. 1911	Quarter-Master.
2 Sept. 1910	Lieutenant M. M. Stevenson	2 Dec. 1912	9 Oct. 1912	—
24 Aug. 1912	Second-Lieutenant A. D. Magnay	25 Aug. 1912	4 Nov. 1913	—
	MEDICAL OFFICERS.			
28 Jan. 1897	Major T. B. Kelly, F.R.C.S.E.	28 Jan. 1909	29 Nov. 1904	—
30 Jan. 1909	Captain B. Gale, M.B.	30 Jan. 1912	16 Mar. 1914	—
	ATTACHED.			
10 Feb. 1893	Honorary-Captain S. E. Skinner	12 Oct. 1910	10 Feb. 1893	Not attached for duty.

NATIVE OFFICERS.

Date of entering Service.	Names.		Jemadar.	Ressaidar.	Risaldar.	Remarks.
	RISALDAR MAJOR.					
1 Apl. 1886	Muhammad Akram Khan (56)	.	1 Nov. 1896	16 Oct. 1902	16 Sept. 1908	Risaldar Major 16 Aug. 1911. I.
	RISALDARS.					
5 July 1881	Ismail Khan Bahadur (56)	.	6 July 1893	1 Apl. 1900	1 Mar. 1906	Order of Br. I., Second class, A.D.C. to Governor Bengal.
	RESSAIDARS.					
13 Apl. 1885	Telemand Khan (56)	.	9 Oct. 1903	—	1 Oct. 1903	—
25 Nov. 1886	Mardan Khan .	.	17 July 1901	1 Mar. 1906	16 Aug. 1911	—
1 Nov. 1891	Ghulam Kadir Rham (56)	.	29 Aug. 1901	10 Nov. 1906	5 Nov. 1912	—
	RESSAIDARS.					
8 Nov. 1889	Ghulam Muhammad Khan (56)	.	16 July 1900	9 Jan. 1909	—	—
16 Jan. 1887	Faiz Muhammad Khan	.	1 Sept. 1902	16 Jan. 1909	—	—
16 Aug. 1899	Syed Raunak Ali Khan	.	18 June 1904	16 Aug. 1911	—	—
14 Jan. 1889	Shaikh Abdul Majid (56)	.	3 Dec. 1904	5 Nov. 1912	—	—
	JEMADARS.					
1 Jan. 1894	Muhammad Ali Khan (1) .	.	1 Mar. 1906	—	—	Woordie Major 1 Apl. 1913.
16 Jan. 1898	Muhammad Ali Khan (2) 45a, (56)	.	1 Nov. 1906	—	—	
1 May 1892	Faujdar Khan .	.	10 Nov. 1906	—	—	—
1 Nov. 1892	Muhammad Ismail Khan (56)	.	1 Oct. 1908	—	—	—
1 May 1892	Mathe Khan	.	1 Oct. 1908	—	—	—
1 May 1898	Muhammad Shafi Khan	.	16 Jan. 1909	—	—	—
1 Aug. 1894	Zabte Khan (56)	.	2 Jan. 1911	—	—	—
1 Feb. 1896	Barkat Khan (56)	.	16 Aug. 1911	—	—	—
13 Apl. 1889	Habibur Rahman Khan, Khan Sahib	.	5 Nov. 1912	—	—	—
1 Mar. 1906	Tahawar Ali	.	5 Nov. 1912	—	—	Bengal Police.

CHAPTER VIII

1902–1914

CENTENARY

THE Regiment was selected in 1902 to send a detachment to England on the occasion of the Coronation of His Majesty the King Emperor. This detachment consisted of Risaldar Major Wazir Ali Khan and nineteen rank and file.

On the 16th February 1903 the Regiment marched from Lucknow to Jhansi in relief. The designation this year was altered to 1st Duke of York's Own Lancers (Skinner's Horse), and it was not without a certain amount of regret that the old title of Bengal Lancers disappeared. The change in nomenclature was, however, necessary under the renumbering scheme in the Indian Army inaugurated by Lord Kitchener.

The year 1903 was a memorable one in the history of the Regiment on account of the celebration of the centenary. Many old pensioners were invited to Jhansi on this occasion, Indian officers, non-commissioned officers, and sowars, and the gathering included mutiny veterans and veterans of many campaigns. Lieutenant Stanley E. Skinner, grandson of the famous founder of the Regiment, was present, and also officers of the 2nd Regiment (3rd Skinner's Horse). The festivities lasted for some days.

The Regiment was detailed specially to attend the manœuvres and review to be held at Rawal Pindi on the occasion of the visit of T.R.H. the Prince and Princess of Wales to India in December 1905. During its stay in Rawal Pindi the Regiment provided numerous escorts for their Royal Highnesses. The Prince visited the Regiment in its camp, and, as its Colonel-in-Chief, presented a silver bowl to the officers' mess to commemorate his visit. On the 20th December H.R.H. the Prince of Wales made the announcement at a State banquet at Gwalior that H.H. the Maharajah Madhorao Scindia of Gwalior had been appointed Honorary Colonel of the Regiment. Major H. L. Roberts was appointed Honorary A.D.C. to H.R.H. the Prince of Wales during his tour in India and received the M.V.O. for his services. Subsequently the Regiment returned to Jhansi. The following year, 1906, Risaldar Major Wazir Ali Khan, Sardar Bahadur, retired after a service of thirty-four years. He was granted the honorary rank of Captain in recognition of his faithful and loyal services.

On the 30th December 1906 the Regiment marched to Agra to take part in the concentration at that place on the occasion of the visit of the Amir of Afghanistan. The review took place on the 12th January 1907, and H.H. the Maharajah Scindia of Gwalior marched past at the head of the Regiment as its Honorary Colonel. About this time Risaldar Major Sher Khan, Sardar Bahadur, was appointed Indian A.D.C. to the G.O.C. Eastern Command.

On the 31st March 1907, Brevet-Colonel C. H. Hayes vacated command of the Regiment and was succeeded by Major C. Davis. In September of the same year the Regiment, having been ordered previously to move in relief to Sirur, was now ordered to Ferozepore. Failure of the monsoon and famine in most districts caused this relief to be cancelled, and the Regiment moved to Lucknow instead.

A tragic incident occurred in the Regiment on the 8th May 1908, when Risaldar Mohamed Kasham Sham, who was acting Risaldar Major, was shot dead. It was supposed to be the deed of a man who had a fancied grievance against him. This Risaldar was a Sadozai and a great-grandson of the Amir Shah Suza. He had settled at Ludhiana. He was Woordie Major for over nine years and rendered invaluable service in that post. An Inspector of Cavalry once remarked that he considered him the best Indian drill instructor he had ever seen. He was a very fine horseman, a fearless and brave man, loyal to his British officers. By his untimely death the Regiment sustained an irreparable loss.

The Regiment left Lucknow by route march on 8th October 1908, and arrived at Dera Ismail Khan on the 4th January 1909. Detachments were furnished for Jandola, Zam, and Jatta posts.

In April 1909, owing to the incursions of Mahsud raiding parties, the garrisons of Zam and Jatta were increased ; a detachment of one squadron at Tank and one or two troops at Mullazai. A column was also sent out along the frontier to the south of Draban. The Tank detachment was withdrawn in June, but the remainder stayed out till November. The movements of these detachments along the frontier checked the incursions of raiders during the hot weather.

On the 6th May 1910 His Majesty King Edward VII died. A telegram of sympathy was sent by the Regiment to King George V., the Colonel-in-Chief, who replied, " The King sincerely thanks all ranks for kind sympathy."

In June 1910 two incidents occurred which are worthy of note as showing the enterprise of an Indian officer. Jemadar Raunaq Ali was in command of the outpost Jatta. He heard that some camels had been looted from a village in the vicinity by tribesmen. He turned out his detachment promptly, pursued the looters and recovered the camels. On another occasion he heard by wire that the Tormanda Militia Post, some ten miles away, was being attacked, and was asking for help. He at once moved out his detachment, half cavalry and half infantry, and made a night march, arriving at Tormanda in the early morning, and relieving the post. The above are good examples of the correct employment of frontier post garrisons and show the initiative and offensive spirit of this detachment.

In October 1910, Major H. L. Roberts, M.V.O., was

appointed Commandant of the 16th Cavalry, and Major C. Bailey, 16th Cavalry, was transferred to the 1st Lancers as second-in-command. About this time Risaldar Major Sher Khan, Sardar Bahadur, who was then A.D.C. to the G.O.C. Northern Army, was transferred to the pension establishment. This Indian officer had a total service of $38\frac{1}{2}$ years and came from a well-known family of Rangars of Rohtak. He served in the second Afghan war and in China, where he was wounded and mentioned in despatches. He was a loyal and highly respected officer and was granted the honorary rank of Captain and a yearly assignment of Rs.600 in addition to the highest pension obtainable.

On the 7th November 1911, on the occasion of a frontier raid, the commanding officer received the following letter of congratulations : " I am directed by the G.O.C. to convey the appreciation of the civil authorities of the prompt manner in which the troops turned out on the occasion of the late raid at Mullang. The G.O.C. is himself very pleased with the work done by the officers of your Regiment."

The Regiment had been ordered to proceed to the Coronation Durbar at Delhi in December. Owing to the failure of the rains and scarcity of fodder, this was cancelled subsequently. Later a representative detachment, consisting of Lieutenant-Colonel C. Davis, Captain Chamberlayne, and 2 Indian officers, and 18 other ranks was sent to Delhi. Captain and Adjutant R.B.C. Raban was appointed Extra A.D.C. to His Majesty the King-Emperor and Risaldar Ismail Khan Orderly Officer. This detachment was present at all ceremonies during the visit of his Majesty to Delhi, and at the review on 14th December formed the escort inside the Royal enclosure. The Indian officers were presented to the King and Queen, and previous to his departure His Majesty presented the second class Order of British India and the Victorian Medal to Risaldar Ismail Khan.

The Regiment won the section tent-pegging at the
5

Native Cavalry meeting at Ambala in February 1912. On the 15th March it moved in relief to Peshawar.   On the 31st March Lieutenant-Colonel C. Davis relinquished command of the Regiment and was succeeded by Lieutenant-Colonel C. Bailey. Major P. Holland Pryor, M.V.O., was appointed second-in-command from the same date.

The year 1913 was uneventful, except for a Cavalry concentration at Gondal near Campbellpore.   The Indian officers in June of this year opened the first Indian officers' mess since the raising of the Regiment 110 years before. This mess flourished and proved to be a great boon, until the amalgamation of the Regiment, and the consequent change of composition in 1921, necessitated its modification into an Indian officers' club.   The earlier days of 1914 were spent in manœuvres in and around Peshawar, and the Regiment was reported on in most flattering terms by various commanders.   Altogether it had attained a very high state of efficiency when the Great War broke out on the 4th August 1914.

CHAPTER IX

1914–1918

ON the outbreak of war the Regiment was made ready for instant service if required. The Indian ranks came forward with a spontaneous and voluntary contribution of Rs.1,000 to H.R.H. the Prince of Wales Relief Fund. This was made up by British officers and Regimental Funds to Rs.1,500 and this sum was forwarded with a letter expressing the wish of all ranks to help in the crisis.

It was the great desire of the Regiment to proceed overseas with one of the Expeditionary Forces which were being mobilised, but the 1st Peshawar Division was to be kept intact to meet eventualities on the Frontier, and so, to their keen disappointment, the Regiment was destined to remain in India. During 1914 and early in 1915 several drafts left for France and eight British officers and several Indian officers of the prewar establishment went to France in 1914 either in Staff employ or as reinforcements. A number of Indian Army Reserve officers joined the Regiment to replace regular officers who had gone to the theatre of war.

On the 7th October 1914 Lieutenant-Colonel C. Bailey relinquished command, having been ordered overseas with Expeditionary Force " B." Lieutenant-Colonel P. Holland Pryor, M.V.O., succeeded to command of the Regiment.

On the 14th April 1915 events on the Mohmand border necessitated a force being sent out to the neighbourhood of Shabkadr. The Regiment formed part of this column

and moved to Shankargarh, near Shabkadr.   On the
16th and 17th April reconnaissances were carried out to
Subhankhwar and Hafiz Kor.   On the 18th April the
column attacked the Mohmands about Hafiz Kor, the
Regiment being on the left flank during the operations.
The force became somewhat heavily engaged and the
Regiment covered the withdrawal of the 72nd Punjabis
and 21st Punjabis.   In these operations Risaldar Faiz Muhammad, a Mussalman-Rajput of Hissar, and Sowar Nishan
Ali, greatly distinguished themselves.   In face of an
advancing enemy these two men went back to search for
two wounded sepoys.   These sepoys were exhausted and
unable to move, so the Risaldar and the sowar lifted them
on their horses and galloped away.   Nishan Ali's horse
stumbled and fell after going 150 yards.   Risaldar Faiz
Muhammad dismounted to help the Sowar and between
them they again got the sepoys on to their horses and
carried them away under a close and heavy fire.   The
Risaldar was awarded the Indian Order of Merit, and
Nishan Ali the Indian Distinguished Service Medal for
their gallant conduct.   The Regiment returned to Peshawar on 23rd April.

On the 29th August the Mohmands again gave trouble
and Headquarters and two Squadrons went out with the
1st Peshawar Division, and other Cavalry Units from Risalpur, to Subhankhwar.   The 31st August to the 3rd September was spent in reconnoitring towards Hafiz Kor, and
on the 4th September the enemy made a heavy night
attack on the camp.   On the 5th September at 7.30 a.m.
the Division moved out to attack the Mohmands.   The
1st Infantry Brigade, to which the Regiment was attached,
was on the left of the line.   One squadron under Major
Macaulay was sent out on the left flank and was at once
engaged by the enemy ; the other squadron was with the
Brigade reserve.   After Artillery preparation the Infantry
attacked in the direction of Hafiz Kor.   The enemy's
strength was estimated at 12,000 men.   At 9.35 a.m.

the Risalpur Cavalry Brigade came up on Major Macaulay's left flank and began a dismounted action ; at the same time the remainder of the 1st Lancers moved up in support of Major Macaulay's squadron. At 10.15 a.m. the Cavalry Brigade fell back. The enemy was threatening this flank and the 1st Lancers became heavily engaged, but supported by two machine guns and a company of the 21st Punjabis they checked the hostile advance.

About 11.10 a.m. two squadrons of the 21st (Empress of India's) Lancers and one squadron of the 14th Jat Lancers (Risalpur Cavalry Brigade) advanced and executed a mounted attack along the left bank of the Michni Canal. It was soon observed that these squadrons were in serious difficulty and suffering from a heavy fire in the vicinity of the Canal. Both squadrons of the 1st Lancers were immediately mounted and, advancing, made a mounted attack along the left bank of the Canal, passing through some of the 21st Lancers en route. As a heavy fire broke out from strong bodies of the enemy who were holding the foothills to the north of the Canal and the crops to the south of it, the regiment retired half a mile, crossed over to the south of the Canal and drove a body of the enemy out of the village of Bires Ghundai, the M.G. section under Lieutenant Magnay covering the advance. Whilst the action at this village was proceeding a Lance-Corporal of the 21st Lancers came up and reported that his Commanding Officer, Lieutenant-Colonel Scriven, had been wounded and was lying among the enemy. The place was located, and Lieutenant-Colonel Holland Pryor, Captain Beaman, and Second-Lieutenant Ewart succeeded in recovering the body under fire from the enemy. Another officer who was mortally wounded and several men of the 21st Lancers were rescued by our sowars. Lieutenant-Colonel Holland Pryor and Captain Beaman each received the D.S.O. for their work on this day ; Second-Lieutenant Ewart received the M.C. Jemadar Ruknuddin and Trumpeter Abdul Majid Khan received the Indian Distinguished Service Medal for acts of gallantry in these operations.

On conclusion of this attack Brigadier-General Dunsterville sent a helio message over: " Well done, 1st Lancers."

As the enemy had now retired to the broken ground, and it was not possible to attack them further, the 1st Lancers withdrew to the main force and at 4 p.m. the troops returned to camp.

On the 8th a second attack was made on the enemy, again towards Hafiz Kor. The Regiment operated on the left flank of the attack and assisted mainly by reconnaissance and dismounted work. They also established communication with the Khyber Rifles about Michni. They received the thanks of General Nigel Woodyat for their work on this day. Until the 30th October, reconnaissances were carried out daily and on the 31st October the force returned to Peshawar. One Squadron remained at Nagoman.

Risaldar Mardan Khan was on the 8th November granted a sword of honour and a killat of Rs.300 in recognition of his good work in connection with recruiting.

In February 1916, Lieutenant-Colonel Holland Pryor vacated command of the Regiment on appointment as additional D.A.G. Army Headquarters, and on the 8th March the 1st Lancers moved to Risalpur.

In May 1916, news was received that Captain (temporary Lieutenant-Colonel) R. B. C. Raban had been killed in France whilst in command of the 13th Royal Scots. This officer had been Adjutant of the Regiment during the four years preceding the war and the Regiment owed much to his unselfish and indefatigable labours. A most popular and capable officer ; his death was deeply regretted by all ranks. The Regiment also lost another regular officer in July 1916 in Lieutenant D. M. Veitch, who was killed whilst flying in France. This officer was interned in Holland early in the war, escaped, was recaptured and escaped again, only to meet his death by a direct hit at 7,000 feet in the Somme battle 1916. He was a very promising young officer and a keen sportsman.

In June 1916 Lieutenant-Colonel F. D. Russell, who had been recalled from a responsible position (A.Q.M.G. 5th Army) in France, took over command of the Regiment.

Throughout the remainder of the war the 1st Lancers continued to serve in the 1st Cavalry Brigade at Risalpur. The ever-present fear of Afghan complications necessitated the presence of regular and complete Regiments on the frontier, although almost all the British officers and a very large percentage of Indian officers and men served at some period in such theatres as France, Salonica, Palestine, Mesopotamia, and East Africa.

In the autumn of 1916 the 1st Lancers again moved out to the Mohmand Border and acted as covering troops to the Infantry, who were employed in the erection of a line of block-houses, connected by a live electric wire from Michni Fort to Abazai. Some good work was carried out and the Commander of the force, after some eulogistic remarks about the Regiment at the end of the operations, wrote, " If they err, it is on the side of boldness, which is the right spirit for Cavalry."

In 1917, when recruiting problems were ever to the fore, the Regiment never had the slightest difficulty in obtaining the requisite numbers of men. The composition was all Mohammedans, and these were sub-divided into one and a half squadrons Punjabis from the Ludhiana and Ferozepore districts, one and a half squadrons Rajput-Mussalmans from Rohtak and Hissar, and one squadron Mohammedans, other than Rajput-Mussalmans, from Rohtak, Hissar, and Gurgaon. At this time the districts of Hoshiarpur and Jullundur were added to the recruiting area, although many men had been drawn from these districts before. When drafts were required for overseas the volunteers always exceeded many times the numbers called for, and there was a general enthusiasm for active service which spoke well for the loyalty and moral of the Regiment. The desire and anxiety of the men to be passed medically fit for these drafts showed the spirit which animated all ranks.

At the end of 1917, two extra squadrons were raised, making six in all, but the lance was excluded in the armament of these two squadrons. They were mounted on a small and indifferent type of country-bred pony which compared unfavourably with the Walers of the Regiment, but except for their horses they were raised and maintained on the Silladar basis. One of these squadrons was eventually sent to form part of the new 40th Cavalry in the Quetta area whilst the other one remained to form a Divisional squadron for the 1st Division.

During the war, 1,346 recruits were enlisted, and at the end of December 1918 the strength of the Regiment, including drafts overseas, was 1,169. Over 70 temporary officers passed through the Regiment during the war. Nearly 1,300 remounts were trained by the Regiment during the war, either to replace normal wastage or to assist the Army generally. The above, as may be seen, implied a great deal of work on the Regimental Training Establishment.

Mention should be made of the good work of Risaldar Major Muhammad Akram Khan. This Indian officer was Risaldar Major throughout the war and the Commandant, Lieutenant-Colonel F. D. Russell, states that " It was largely, if not entirely, due to this officer's fine qualities of all sorts that the Regiment remained in so good and keen a condition throughout this critical period." He was awarded the 2nd class Order of British India for his services, later on receiving the 1st class Order and the honorary rank of Captain.

Major A. Chamberlayne, after serving in France, raised a temporary battalion of the 72nd Punjabis, and was killed in action at the head of it at the Ahnai Tangi in Waziristan on the 14th January 1920. He was highly spoken of by General Climo, and was a great loss both to the Regiment and to the 72nd Punjabis. He is buried in the cemetery at Jandola.

The following is the final entry in the records of the Regiment for the Great War, and is well worth quoting here :

" In closing this account of the work of the 1st Lancers in the Great War, it is only fair to the Regiment to call attention to the manner in which, in spite of its disappointment at not being privileged, owing to its position in the 1st (Frontier) Cavalry Brigade in India, to proceed overseas as a unit, and also in spite of the very heavy and continuous drain on its strength of British and Indian officers, trained soldiers and horses, it maintained its reputation as a trained Cavalry Regiment in India. It proceeded three times on field service to the Mohmand Border and its annual inspection reports were always excellent, the last report in 1918 being to the effect that it had maintained its pre-war standard."

A list of honours gained by British officers, Indian officers, and other ranks during the Great War and subsequent operations are given in Appendix D.

CHAPTER X

1918–1921

THIRD AFGHAN WAR—ORDERED TO PERSIA

On the conclusion of the Armistice in November 1918, the strength of the Regiment was gradually reduced, and the remaining extra squadron which had been raised was disbanded, the horses being sold by auction and the men being either absorbed or discharged. Leave was opened in April 1919 on a fairly generous scale, the irreducible minimum being reached to carry on musketry and internal security duties. Several pre-war officers had now returned and the squadrons had their permanent squadron commanders for the first time for four years. A large number of temporary British officers were still present, the numbers being gradually reduced by demobilisation.

At the end of April, concurrent with unrest in the Punjab, the Amir Habibullah of Afghanistan was murdered and ominous reports began to come in from over the Border. Finally, on May 5th, war broke out with Afghanistan. General mobilisation was ordered about midday on May 6th, and the 1st Lancers left Risalpur at one and a half hours' notice at 8 p.m. the same evening. A march of over forty-two miles was carried out that night, the Regiment arriving next day at 11 a.m. at Shaghai Thana, twelve miles north-west of Peshawar, in order to watch the exit of the Mullagori road from the Khyber. Owing to leave and furlough, the total strength of the Regiment was 260, with 11 British officers, Brevet-Colonel F. D. Russell commanding. A nucleus was left behind to form the depot and bring foward the leave and furlough men when they returned. The horses were " soft " at the time and a march of forty-two miles in fifteen hours under heavy marching order was no mean performance, considering the heat, and the fact that the Regiment had to remain for two hours under saddle at Peshawar drawing ammunition and certain stores. There were no casualties amongst either men or horses. One squadron took over Shaghai post ; the rest of the Regiment went into perimeter camp south of Burj Shahi.

On the 11th May orders were received at 2 p.m. to join the remainder of the Risalpur Cavalry Brigade at Jamrud, where they had marched subsequently to the departure of the 1st Lancers. The route followed was via Shaghai Thana and thence along the track south to Jamrud, which was reached that evening. A large proportion of transport carts had been ordered in that day to Peshawar to draw supplies and so there was considerable difficulty in transporting kits and stores in this move. On 12th May the Regiment halted at Jamrud.

In the meantime a portion of the 1st Peshawar Division had been in action against the Afghans about Landi Kotal and Landi Khana and had driven the enemy off the Bagh Springs and the heights commanding them. Lieutenant-General Sir A. Barrett, who was now in command of the troops on the Khyber Line, decided to clear the enemy off the hills on either side of the Khyber Pass as far as the Northern exit beyond Haft Chah Post, and then to pass the 1st Cavalry Brigade through to seize Dakka on the 13th May. The Cavalry Brigade left Jamrud at 4.30 a.m. on that date, the 1st Lancers forming the advanced guard, " B " Squadron under Major Sexton leading. The force reached Landi Khana by 10.30 a.m. where delay was caused owing to the restricted watering facilities. At 11.30 a.m. the 1st Lancers, with three armoured cars and two machine guns attached, were sent forward to seize Dakka and to reconnoitre the Dakka plain as far as Robat Fort and Sherabad Cantonment. The Regiment debouched from the pass without hindrance. " A " Squadron (Major Wetherall) was detached to the right and " C " Squadron

(Major Muirhead) to the left, whilst the remainder of the detachment moved direct on Dakka down the main road. The village was occupied without resistance, two prisoners being taken and some valuable correspondence seized in the late headquarters of the Afghans. On the west of the village was the remains of the Afghan camp from which they had fled, after a bombing raid the previous day. The Mohmands from the other side of the Kabul River had crossed later and completed the desolation. The stench from unburied horses which had been killed at their standings was very great, and the confusion of stores, ammunition, and equipment which lay scattered over the whole area defies description. A gun was taken by " C " Squadron and is now in the officers' mess, Skinner's Horse.

Meanwhile, "A" Squadron proceeded on reconnaissance to Kam Dakka and reported all clear ; " C " Squadron reconnoitring Robat Fort and Sherabad Cantonment and thence moving round Point 1995 north-west of Sherabad) where the depth of water close up to the Cliff prevented further advance. These reconnaissances were sniped from the north side of the river and from the hills to the south of the river, but no serious resistance was encountered. One of the missions of the left squadron was to report on the boat bridge to Lalpura, but this was found to be dismantled. The remainder of the 1st Cavalry Brigade arrived during the afternoon and the whole went into camp south of, and adjoining, Dakka village.

On the 14th May a reconnaissance under Major Muirhead was sent via Robat and Sherabad to the Khurd Khyber defile, where the enemy was found to be holding the entrance to the pass, in small numbers. The ground was bad and an action at long range was opened. During the firing Afghan envoys flying a white flag came down the road in a car. They had come from Jalalabad with letters from the Amir proposing peace, and were sent finally to Landi Kotal. A further envoy was brought in later by an evening patrol under Jemadar Ibrar Hassan. Risaldar Major Muhammad Akram Khan, an Afghan by descent, was this day appointed temporary political officer to the force, and was engaged in translating and collating correspondence found in Dakka village, and other work in connection with the inhabitants. Elements of the 1st Infantry Brigade joined the Dakka force in the afternoon.

On the 15th May the King's Dragoon Guards took over the reconnaissance work. In the evening a reconnaissance of the 1st Lancers was ordered to proceed past Robat and Sherabad to look for any possible ford in the Kabul River. As fighting seemed probable, two troops were sent out under Major Sexton and Captain Lawson. Major Sexton left Captain Lawson with most of his men as a support at Robat and proceeded with Risaldar Gholam Muhammad Khan, a trumpeter, and a few men, past Sherabad. He was fired on but went on trying several places in the river. Having crossed the smaller channels, his horse was finally swept off its feet in the main stream and he was fired on hotly at 400 yards range. To add to his difficulties his saddle slipped round and eventually he and his trumpeter, who had come to his assistance, were compelled to withdraw.

On the 16th May a mixed force was despatched through the Khurd Khyber defile to clear up the situation in the direction of Girdi and Hazarno. When west of Girdi this force encountered strong opposition from over 4,000 Afghans and with difficulty withdrew to camp. The Afghans then occupied the heights west of Dakka village, and, bringing a battery of mountain guns into action, shelled the camp at 2,000 yards range. The camp, being in the open plain, afforded little cover and one of the earlier shells wounded Major Wetherall and killed several horses. All the animals of the brigade were then moved to a nullah east of the camp which gave good cover. The enemy pressed on to the rear vicinity of the camp and a very hot fire was kept up all the afternoon by both sides, which rendered any movement in the camp next to impossible. Amongst the casualties this day was Dafadar Hardiya Khan, the regimental signalling Dafadar, who was shot through the neck and died instantly.   This N.C.O. had, almost single-handed, during the latter stages of the Great War, worked the signallers up to a high standard of efficiency, and his death was a great loss to the Regiment.   At dusk the firing died down and at 9 p.m. some of the enemy made a rush at the western face of the camp ; this was checked by well-controlled fire.   The behaviour of all ranks on this very trying day was exemplary.   There was little cover from the enemy's fire, and the necessary movements of clearing the camp of horses and transport under a hot fire was carried out with a coolness which was highly praiseworthy.

On the 17th May the battle recommenced at dawn, the Infantry of the force attacking the heights to the west of the camp.   The 1st Lancers sent a detachment to the south-west of the camp to secure the left flank of the attack, and also one squadron was moved down the Robat road, but was unable to proceed further than a small enclosure west of Dakka village.   The infantry attack was held up short of the crest and the Regiment with other cavalry units was called upon to be prepared to move up the hills on foot to support the Infantry.   This, however, never materialised, as the arrival of reinforcements, with howitzers, from the Khyber caused the enemy to evacuate his positions at 2 p.m.   That night detachments of the 1st Lancers with other units of the Cavalry Brigade took over the pickets around Haft Chah post at the exit of the Khyber; the next day the whole force moved into a new and more sanitary camp between Robat and Sherabad.

Preparations were made to advance to Jalalabad at the beginning of June, but these were subsequently cancelled and the Dakka force remained about Sherabad throughout the rest of the operations.   Columns were despatched frequently on foraging and punitive expeditions, starting sometimes before dawn and returning the same evening. Daily reconnaissances went out towards Girdi and east and south of Dakka. Convoy escorts also gave plenty of work for the Cavalry.

The climatic conditions were exceedingly trying both for men and horses. The heat was intense and dust storms blew all day and sometimes all night ; the main relaxation was the bathing in the Kabul River, which enabled the troops to get a short respite from dust and heat. The Cavalry was called upon to take over, construct, and man permanent pickets to the south-east of the camp; with this and the usual camp fatigues, water-pumping parties, and road-construction parties, in addition to tactical operations, the men were kept very busy. Notwithstanding all this the health of the Regiment remained very good, and all work was carried out in good heart. The furlough and leave men arrived at Dakka towards the end of May, thus bringing the unit up to war strength.

The protracted peace negotiations terminated the campaign in October and the Regiment returned to Risalpur on the 22nd of that month. On the 1st November the 1st Lancers moved to Delhi by rail, three squadrons going into camp at Kingsway and one squadron into the old cavalry lines, large numbers of the men proceeding on furlough. Rumours were abroad that the Regiment would shortly go to Palestine, but definite orders were received to move to Lucknow. Whilst at Delhi, honorary Captain Stanley Skinner, before a full parade, presented the favourite sword of Colonel James Skinner, C.B., to the officer commanding the 1st Skinner's Horse " upon trust for the officers for the time being of the Regiment to be kept in the Mess in memory of his grandfather."

Colonel F. D. Russell had left the Regiment in July 1919 to take up a staff appointment and the temporary command had devolved on Major D. I. Macaulay. On July 7th 1920, Lieutenant-Colonel Rivett Carnac of the 14th Jat Lancers was appointed Commandant, but reverted to his own Regiment on the 1st December 1920, being succeeded by Lieutenant-Colonel L. Dening.   The Regiment was warned for service in North Persia to relieve the Guides Cavalry at Kasvin, and embarked at Bombay on the 24th December 1920 for Basra.   Proceeding up the river to Amara, it halted there for some days, when, on the change of policy and consequent reduction of the garrison in Persia, it received orders to return to India, where it arrived at the beginning of February, being quartered at Lucknow.

At this time the scheme of conversion to non-silladar, and amalgamation with the 3rd Skinner's Horse, came into operation, and reduction of personnel and the settling up with silladars was the order of the day.   In May 1921 the 1st Lancers entrained for Sialkot to link up with the 3rd Horse, the command of the amalgamated Regiment being taken over by Lieutenant-Colonel E. Conway-Gordon, C.I.E.   Thus after over one hundred years of separation the two Regiments united again, under the title of the " 1st Duke of York's Own Skinner's Horse."

PART III

THE 2ND CORPS OR THE 3RD SKINNER'S HORSE

" Afghanistan " ; " Ghuznee," 1839 ; " Kelat " ; " Maharajpore " ;
" Moodkee " ; " Ferozeshah " ; "Aliwal " ; " Kandahar, 1880 " ;
"Afghanistan, 1879–80 " ; " Punjab Frontier " ; " The Great War " ;
" France and Flanders, 1914–15–16 " ; " Baluchistan, 1918 " ; " The
Third Afghan War."

Extract from the Bengal Army List "1823"

4TH REGIMENT (OR BADDELEY'S) LOCAL HORSE

MEEMUCH

Rank and Names.	Army Rank.	Remarks.
Major W. C. Baddeley, 24th N.I. .	18 Jan. 1823	Commandant.
Bt.-Captain G. W. Moseley, 19th N.I.	24 May 1821	Second in Command.
Bt.-Captain T. R. Macqueen, 23rd N.I.	1 Mar. 1823	Adjutant.
Cornet C. D. Dawkins, 2nd Light Cavalry	4 July 1821	
		Assistant Surgeon.

CHAPTER XI

1819–1841

TOWARDS the end of 1819 the Corps marched to Neemuch, where it was to be permanently stationed. In 1821 Major Robert Skinner died, and was succeeded in command of the Corps by Captain W. C. Baddeley. The name of the Corps was then changed to " Baddeley's Frontier Horse." In 1823 Regiments of Local Horse were given numbers, this Regiment becoming the 4th. In 1824 Captain Carmichael Smyth, of the 3rd Light Cavalry, Brigade Major of the Meywaur Field Force, was nominated to the command of the Corps. In 1830 the Corps was transferred to the Saugor District, where the men greatly distinguished themselves in the seizure of Thugs, for which service the Government presented the Corps with a piece of plate, which is now in the Mess.

The following letter explains this presentation :

*To F. C. Smith, Esq., Agent Governor-General, Saugor and
Nurbuddah Territories.*

SIR,

I have the honour to request that you will solicit the sanction of Government to a charge of 300 rupees for the purchase of a silver " Pawn-Dawn " to be presented to the native officers and men of the 4th Local Horse, under the command of Captain Carmichael Smyth, to mark the high sense entertained of their valuable services during the time they were stationed in this District, in aid of our attempts to suppress Thug associations.

They were, from this central point of Saugor, often

detached with parties into the District of Oude, the Dooab, Delhi, Rajpootaun, Goozeraut and Gaudeish, and employed in situations of great danger and difficulty, and in all situations, and under all circumstances, they discharged the duties entrusted to them to our satisfaction and in numerous instances excited our admiration !

There were many instances in which I felt desirous of applying for some special mark of favour, but they seemed to be all animated by so much zeal, and so anxious to discharge well the duties entrusted to them, that I thought it would be better to make no distinctions, and to content myself with promising that I would, through you, bring their conduct to the notice of the Government, and request for the whole collectively some mark of distinction that might tend to give the Corps pride in the recollection of the service rendered by them to a cause so interesting to humanity.

If, in addition to this charge, Government should sanction the engraving of some suitable inscription upon the article it would certainly tend to do so, and be a source of satisfaction as well to the Corps in general, as to the individuals employed under us.

I have the honour to be, etc., etc.,
(Signed) W. H. SLEEMAN,
Political Assistant Agent Governor-General,
SAUGOR, 11*th April* 1834.

In 1834 the Corps was transferred to Bareilly, where its strength was increased from 800 to 1,000 men. In 1838 the Corps was again back at Neemuch, but towards the latter part of that year received orders to march to Hansi and join the 1st Corps. The two corps were to form the 2nd Cavalry Brigade, under Brigadier-General James Skinner, in the Army of the Indus, which was assembled at Ferozepore in November for operations against Afghanistan. Major Alexander, of the 5th Light Cavalry, now succeeded Major Carmichael Smyth in command of the Corps, the latter returning to take up command of his own Regiment, the 3rd Light Cavalry. News, however, having been received of the withdrawal of the Persian Army, which had been besieging Herat, it was decided to reduce the strength of the Army of the Indus. The 2nd Cavalry Brigade was broken up, and only the 2nd Corps and one Risalah of the 1st Corps accompanied the Expeditionary Force, a service for which they volunteered. On the 10th December the Army marched from Ferozepore, and arrived at Rohri in Sindh on the 24th January 1839, where it was joined by the Bombay troops marching from Karachi under Sir John Keane. The Indus was crossed by a bridge of boats, and Shikarpur reached on the 20th February. Sir John Keane was now in command of the Army, and the march on Quetta through the Bolan Pass began. When the Corps was advancing through the Bolan Pass, Woordie Major Shahamut Khan (Baluch), whose portrait is now in the Mess, followed a party of Baluchis into the hills, and after a long and difficult chase killed one of their chiefs in single combat, which gained for him the applause of the whole Army. Quetta was reached on the 26th March, and after a fortnight's delay the Army proceeded through the Khojak Pass to Kandahar. During the march to Kandahar, men and horses suffered great privations through scarcity of provisions. Being Local Horse, they were not entitled under the existing regulations to obtain grain for their horses from the commissariat, and it was unobtainable locally owing to the famine conditions which prevailed. In spite of the fact that Sir John Keane did not grant them grain from the commissariat until he had obtained the opinion of a committee of Field Officers expressing the necessity of the measure, yet the Governor-General, in Council, countermanded the measure as soon as it was referred to him. The duties that fell to the Corps were mainly those of escorting convoys and baggage, and protecting cattle at graze. Amongst other exploits was that of Risaldar

Azim Khan, in bringing in the convoy of Lohanee merchants to Kandahar with supplies of grain for the Army. It was due to the bravery, firmness, and decision of Azim Khan that this convoy of 1,500 camels was not carried off for the service of the enemy. For his conduct on this occasion, Risaldar Azim Khan was presented by Sir John Keane with a handsome pair of pistols.

Extract from the Bengal Army List " July 1839 "

4TH REGIMENT OF LOCAL HORSE

(With the Army of the Indus)

Rank and Names.	Army Rank.	When Appointed.	Remarks.
Captain W. Alexander, 5th L.C. . .	30 May 1830	17 Oct. 1833	Commandant.
Lieutenant T. Walker, 1st N.I. . .	24 Nov. 1827	8 Dec. 1829	Second in Command.
Lieutenant W. H. Ryves, 61st N.I. .	11 Oct. 1838	27 Sept.1838	Adjutant.
Assistant Surgeon J. Worral, M.D. .	14 Aug. 1825	3 July 1827	In Medical charge.
Ressaldar Shaik h Noor Bux . .	1 May 1837	—	Bahadur.

The march on Kabul was resumed on the 27th June. On the 21st July the Army arrived before Ghazni, which was found to be held in considerable strength; on the 22nd Ghazni was taken by storm.

On the 30th July the Army moved on towards Kabul. On its approach the Amir, Dost Muhammad, fled from the capital. A lightly equipped detachment under Captain Outram was despatched to the Bamian Pass in pursuit, Lieutenant W. H. Ryves, the Adjutant, the Medical Officer, and certain volunteers from the Regiment formed part of this detachment. On the 7th August Shah Shuja made his state entry into Kabul. This concluded the first phase of the Afghan War, and arrangements were begun for the withdrawal of the greater part of the Army to India.

Two Risalahs of the Regiment under Captain Thomas
Walker remained with the Army of Occupation in Afghanistan. Walker had been appointed Adjutant in 1829,
and it was during this campaign that his zeal and gallantry
won for him the admiration of the whole Army. He had
with him the Risalahs of Iman Ali Khan and Azim Khan.
Of Imam Ali Khan Walker writes :

" I consider him ten times better than any of the other
officers, and every European officer he has served under
praises him up to the skies. Though apparently un-
wieldy he is as active as possible, as brave as a lion, and
in action has never left my side, and in every difficulty
I have always placed the greatest confidence in him."

Of the men he writes :

" If the Government would only be liberal to the men
I would much like to command the Regiment in Afghanistan. I venture to say with 800 of them we would thrash
as many Afghans as chose to appear before us. The Yellow
Boys are regular ' Dreadnoughts,' and the stories of their
bravery related to me by the different officers with whom
they have been detached almost beat what I have witnessed
with my own eyes, and this is most gratifying."

In November 1839 Walker's Risalahs accompanied
Major-General Willshire's column against Mehrab Khan,
the Baluch Khan of Kalat.

The force was attacked by the enemy's horse as it approached Kalat on the 13th November, and the skir-
mishing continued to within a short distance of the town.
The Fort was stormed and captured after a brave struggle,
the Khan and several Sirdars being slain.

All Corps which advanced beyond the Bolan Pass were
granted permission to bear the word "Afghanistan "
on their Colours and appointments, and those which were
present at the capture of Ghazni and Kalat were permitted
to inscribe the names of those places also, and a medal
was afterwards given for the capture of Ghazni.

For their services in this war, Major Alexander and

Captain Walker received the Order of the Durani Empire. Risaldar Azim Khan's services were brought to the notice of the Governor-General, who appointed him an A.D.C. He was the first Indian officer to be appointed an A.D.C. to the Governor-General.

The Headquarters of the Regiment formed part of the force that escorted Hyder Khan to Ferozepore, where it remained for three years. In a letter dated the 20th March 1840, General Thackwell, commanding the Cavalry Division, says :

" The 4th Local Horse proved themselves a most useful, hardworking, and brave set of men, . . . and their losses and privations were greater than any other men of the service as they received but little assistance from the commissariat."

When it is remembered that the Regiment was a Local Corps raised for specific duties in a certain district in India, and had volunteered for foreign service in Afghanistan, it is surprising how the authorities failed to meet promptly their very legitimate claim for assistance in the matter of rations.

From Kalat, Captain Walker with his Risalahs returned to Kandahar, where they formed part of the garrison under the celebrated General Nott.

In April 1840 the Ghilzais broke out in open revolt against the British and Shah Shuja. A column under Captain Anderson, Bengal Artillery, was despatched from Kandahar toward Kalat-i-Ghilzai to suppress this rising. Walker and one Risalah formed part of this column. On the 16th the enemy were brought to battle at Tazi, and after an action remarkable for the gallantry displayed on both sides, the Ghilzais were driven in confusion to the refuge of their mountain fastnesses. This operation entailed long marches and severe fighting ; Walker writes :

" I never did more for my masters before nor do I think I could possibly go through the same again. The fatigue of body was as nothing compared with that of the mind,

and often when lying on the ground asleep with my men
have I started up thinking we were attacked. For the
whole month we never slept without our clothes and our
arms at our sides."

In the beginning of September 1840 Walker started
with Major-General Nott from Kandahar for Kalat, via
Quetta. The son of the Khan who had been killed when
General Willshire captured Kalat had retaken possession
of his father's fortress, and our Army was ordered to attack
the place again. Walker writes :

" I have got my Rissalahs into beautiful order, fine
young horses, as sleek and as fat as butter, but ere we
reach Kalat I fear they will be skin and bone, as forage
is very scarce, the rebels having plundered the whole of
the Shawl Valley. There is neither lucerne nor bhoossa
to be got."

Again, on the 1st November 1840 Walker writes :

" I have been sadly floored ever since leaving Kalat,
and this is the first day I have been able to sit up. Dysentery attacked me, after the fever, and though I was only
delirious three or four days, it left me so weak, I could not
sit up. Then I was attacked with violent pains in the head.
I am reduced to skin and bone, and looking like a ghost.
I have now suffered three attacks of fever and dysentery.
The doctors say it is caused by constant knocking about,
and exposure to the bitter cold at night and morning, and
to the sun till two or three p.m., for we seldom get into
our tents till that hour ! I ought to go away, but I must
try and hold on until my men are relieved."

On the 20th February 1841 Walker writes :

" The doctors want me to go off to Bombay, and thence
to sea, but as I am now convalescent, I do not like to leave
my men in this country. . . . Since the Regiment (the
Headquarters of it) returned to India, the Government
have behaved a little more liberally, in granting some of
the requests we made, but not without a great deal of
correspondence on the subject.

" It is a great pity the men were not treated better when they were on foreign service, and so hardworked—the hardship of their case was so clear to everyone, that the commiseration they met with, added fuel to the fire, and a bad feeling was created towards Government, which it will take a long time to do away with.

" Our men are great favourites, and deservedly so, with the General (Nott), and I get on famously with him also."

Again he wrote from Kalat-i-Ghilzai on the 30th July :

" The hard work, exposure to heat and cold, and anxiety of mind I have suffered has much injured my strong constitution. . . . I am delighted now, however, that you got the Regiment employed on this service, as it has done the men the world of good, and proved to everyone what stuff they are made of.

" They have now gained a name for themselves which they can never lose, and are equally respected both by friends and foes ! "

Early in April 1841 trouble again broke out with the Ghilzais. Extract from *The Times*, 6th November 1841 :

" DEFEAT OF THE GHILZAIS.—The enemy continued increasing until the 5th instant, and kept a strict watch upon our troops, day and night. The numbers at length apparently amounted to 3,000 men, and the Ghilzais having made an attack upon the Grasscutters of the camp, the Rissalah of Local Horse (the 4th), under Captain Walker, dashed at them first, and cut up about 200. A troop of the 5th Light Cavalry, under Lieutenant Bazett, attacked another party, and killed some twenty of them.

" We regret to say that Lieutenant Bazett was very severely wounded by a musket shot through the thigh. Captain Walker's horse was shot dead under him, but he escaped."

In August the temporary submission of the Ghilzais was gained by a decided success at Karutu near the Saighan Pass, in which action Walker's Risalahs took part.

Just before the insurrection broke out at Kabul in

November 1841, Walker arrived there with some State prisoners he had escorted from Kandahar.

On the 23rd November during the disastrous action on the Bemaru Heights, Walker received a mortal wound in a heroic effort to cover the withdrawal of the Infantry. With infinite exertion he rallied a few horsemen and charged an overwhelming host of Afghan Cavalry, thus saving our panic-stricken force from a general massacre.

Walker's death was deeply mourned by the garrison of Kabul. He had won for himself a great name throughout the Army, and it is almost remarkable that every memoir written on this campaign mentions Walker in connection with some feat of gallantry.

Imam Ali's Risalah marched out of Kabul on the 6th January 1842 at the head of Elphinstone's ill-fated Army. The story of the disastrous retreat from Kabul is well known, and it will be remembered that Dr. Brydon was the only man of that Army to reach Jalalabad. The whole of Imam Ali's troop did not perish ; individual men managed to regain India after the arrival of Pollock's Army of Revenge at Kabul. Being Mohammedans, many were spared from the general massacre, but of those who regained India, a large percentage were maimed for life from the effects of frost-bite. A grandson of one of the survivors was enlisted in the Regiment in 1914.

CHAPTER XII

1842–1856

MAHARAJPORE—THE FIRST SIKH WAR—MUDKI—FEROZESHAH—ALIWAL.

ON the 15th November 1842 the Regiment moved into camp to form part of the Army of Reserve which was then assembling on the plains round Ferozepore, under the Commander-in-Chief, Sir Jasper Nicholls, in person. This force had been collected to overawe the Sikhs and cover the withdrawal of the Army returning from Afghanistan. The Regiment was brigaded with the 16th Light Dragoons and the 7th Light Cavalry, under the command of Brigadier Cureton. On the morning of the 9th December the whole Army was paraded to receive the Governor-General, Lord Ellenborough ; and in the afternoon there was a display of feats of skill and horsemanship before His Excellency by the men of the Irregular Cavalry, in which the greater number of prizes bestowed fell to the troopers of the Regiment. On the morning of the 17th the Army was drawn up in review order to receive the illustrious garrison of Jalalabad. On the 18th and 19th General Pollock's two Divisions crossed the river. On the 23rd General Nott's Army crossed, and moved into camp on the parade-ground in Ferozepore. They brought with them the famous gates of Somnath. On the 31st the whole of the troops in the vicinity of Ferozepore were reviewed by His Excellency the Commander-in-Chief. The whole of this period had been one of gay festivity, but on the 5th January 1843 the days of the Indian Field of the Cloth of Gold came to an end.

The Regiment received orders to march to Bareilly via Delhi, which latter station they reached on the 3rd February. At Delhi there was a repetition on a smaller scale of the scene at Ferozepore, parades and durbars being the order of the day. On the 19th February the march was continued to Bareilly, where the Regiment arrived on the 7th March.

Captain Oldfield succeeded Major Alexander in command of the Regiment during this year, with Captain Cavenagh and Lieutenant Ryves as Second in Command and Adjutant.

In October the Regiment was warned to join the Army of Exercise to be assembled at Agra, and on the 9th November commenced its march to Muttra, where it was to join its Brigade, the 16th Lancers and the 10th Light Cavalry. Shortly after arrival at Agra the 16th Lancers and the 4th Irregular Cavalry were reviewed by the Commander-in-Chief. It was a hard test, as there were several recruits and young horses and the Corps had been scattered throughout the hot weather, some of the detachments only rejoining Headquarters a day or two before the march.

The concentration of troops at Agra had been intended as a demonstration against Gwalior; but it did not produce the beneficial effect which had been anticipated, and eventually in December the Army was moved forward to attack Gwalior.

The following account of the operations is taken from the memoirs of Captain Cavenagh (afterwards General Sir Orfeur Cavenagh), who lost a leg at the battle of Maharajpur.

On the 15th December the Regiment commenced to march to the Chumbal, having previously despatched four troops as escort to the battering train. After halting for two or three days at Dholpur, the right wing, under the Commander-in-Chief, crossed the river on the 22nd and marched to Higona, which was reached on the 26th.

On the 27th a reconnoitring party escorted by a detachment of the Regiment was fired upon. Galloping back under the cannonade, one of the officers dropped his forage cap, when a trooper quietly pulled up, dismounted, picked it up, and returned it to him. The next day orders were issued for the advance on Gwalior. As in addition to having six troops absent on detached duty the Regiment had been called upon to furnish a detachment of a hundred picked troopers to be employed as a body-guard to the Governor-General, the strength of the Corps was reduced to two weak troops.

Cavenagh writes :

" On the morning of the 29th we paraded at gun-fire and joined our Brigade. . . . At about 7.30 a.m. we arrived opposite the walled village of Omedgurh, and I was directed to station one of our troops so as to defeat any attempt to plunder the baggage or to take us in rear on the part of any body of the enemy by which it might be occupied. I accordingly posted the main body out of musket shot, and in front of the only gateway through which Cavalry could have made their exit, with videttes placed at intervals so as to command a view of the four sides of the village. I had hardly stationed the last vidette, when the Mahrattas opened fire upon our advancing columns, and, anxious to overtake the Regiment, I made a short cut, and, followed by my orderlies, dashed under the walls, which I then discovered to be crowded with the matchlock men, and was therefore delighted when I found myself again on the high road with a whole skin. I speedily resumed my post with the Regiment. As we advanced the cannonade rapidly increased in vigour, and after passing the village of Mingrowlee, the enemy's batteries became distinctly visible in the direction of Maharajpur, playing upon the heads of our Infantry Brigades, which were now observed to our left, deploying into line. Previous to the attack our Brigade was formed up, and moved steadily onwards, parallel to the Infantry, and

covering their right flank. It was a splendid sight to see
the latter marching in parade order across a plain swept
by the fire of the Mahratta Artillery. They were, however,
troops that no danger could daunt, and apparently not a
check of even a moment's duration was sustained during
their admirable advance. Upon arriving within a few
hundred yards of Maharajpur a fire was opened upon our
Brigade from two guns posted on the left of the village.
We were accordingly halted, pending the operations on
our left being brought to a successful termination.

Extract from the Bengal Army List " July 1844 "

4TH REGIMENT OF IRREGULAR CAVALRY

"Afghanistan " ; " Ghuznee " ; " Maharajpoor " ; 2 Rissalahs " Kelat."

BAREILLY.—Arrived 7th March 1843.

Detachments at Meerut, Lucknow, etc.

Rank, Names, and Corps.	Army Rank.	When Appointed.	Remarks.
Lieutenant-Colonel C. E. T. Oldfield, C.B., 5th L.C.	30 April 1844	23 Dec. 1842	Commandant. Leave, S.C., to 7th Nov.
Major R. Cautley, 10th L.C.	30 April 1844	27 Mar. 1844	Acting Commandant.
Lieutenant O. Cave-nagh, 32nd N.I.	13 Jan. 1842	8 Oct. 1844	Second in Command.
Ensign R. G. Mayne, 59th N.I. (attached to the Kelat-i-Ghilzie Regiment)	10 Aug. 1840	10 July 1844	Acting Adjutant.
Assistant Surgeon F. C. Henderson, M.D.	10 Feb. 1831	25 Feb. 1840	—

The 4th Regiment of Irregular Cavalry consists of 8 Ressallahs, with
1 Woordie Major, 1 Nakeeb, 1 Persian writer, 2 native Doctors, 4 Ressaldars, 4 Ressaidars, 8 Naib Ressaldars, 8 Jemadars, 8 Kote Duffadars,
72 Duffadars, 8 Nishanburdars, 6 Trumpeters, 2 Nuggarchies, 680 Sowars.

" In the meantime all eyes were fixed on the movements
of the 3rd and 5th Brigades of Infantry ; undismayed by
a heavy cannonade, which mowed them down by sections,

they had now diminished the distance which separated them from their foes to within a few yards.   For a second there was a halt ; the next the bayonets glistened as they were brought to the charge ; a British cheer pealed through the air, a rush, a last vain struggle, and the batteries of Maharajpur were won.   A desperate resistance was, however, still offered by the Battalions posted in the village, and when their ammunition was expended they gallantly opposed the sword and shield to the British bayonet.   It was but a vain effort ; the superior prowess of our troops finally prevailed, and they were driven from every post they attempted to maintain ; but not until the village had caught fire, and several of the combatants perished in the flames.   As at this time Her Majesty's 16th Lancers broke into open column, preparatory to an advance on Choundah, I was despatched to ascertain what orders had been issued relative to our movements.   Whilst, however, I was still in search of the Brigadier, the two troops of Horse Artillery detached themselves from the Brigade and galloped to the front.   Perceiving that they were escorted by the 4th Irregular Cavalry, I turned, and as we swept round the flank of the burning village we obtained a view of the whole battlefield . . . After we had been in this position for about twenty minutes, an aide-de-camp rode up bearing orders from the Commander-in-Chief for the Regiment, or rather troop, to advance.

" The command was gallantly responded to, but I was debarred the good fortune of sharing in the honour of the charge, for at that moment, by a discharge from a battery under some trees immediately in our front, my horse was mortally wounded and my left leg carried away ; my poor charger upon being struck reared up, and for a second remained poised in the air.   I vainly endeavoured to dismount, the whole of my side being for the moment paralysed by the shock experienced from the blow of the round shot ; and then with a crash we fell together to the ground. After some little exertion I managed to extricate myself from my dangerous position, when, for the first time, I perceived that my leg had been severed a little above the ankle. The troop had pushed on, but my two orderlies had dismounted and were standing by my side. Hardly had I unloosed my silk necktie and bound it tightly round the wounded limb, ere Henderson also reached the spot where I was lying, and at once applied a tourniquet.

" The weak troop of the 4th Regiment Irregular Cavalry engaged, behaved with great gallantry; in the charge that took place after I was wounded, they broke an Infantry square, capturing its colours and silencing two guns, the native adjutant, Mir Hidyat Ali, and two of his brothers particularly distinguishing themselves. The first named, observing some slight wavering amongst the troopers, rushed forward in a line with the European officers, calling out to the men not to desert their leaders. One brother was the standard-bearer of the troop, and, as he galloped up to the square, made an appeal to his comrades to follow their colour, which he flung inside; he was severely wounded whilst breaking through the Mahratta ranks."

The Commander-in-Chief, Sir Hugh Gough, in his despatch says :

" I was greatly gratified by a spirited charge made by Major Oldfield, of the 4th Irregular Cavalry, who had been left to cover Major Alexander's troop of Horse Artillery, and who charged by my orders a considerable body of the enemy's Infantry. Two guns and three Standards awarded this charge."

In this action two sowars were killed, Captain Cavenagh severely wounded, Dafadars Jaffir Ali and Asghur Ali and Sowar Pir Bux wounded. Naib Risaldar Mir Hidyat Ali and Dafadars Asghur Ali and Jaffir Ali received the 3rd Class Order of Merit, and Risaldar Jowahir Singh the 2nd Class Order of British India with the title of Bahadur.

7

A bronze medal made from the material of the captured guns was issued to all ranks engaged in the campaign, and the several Corps engaged in the battles of Maharajpur and Paniar were permitted to inscribe those names on their Colours and appointments. Subsequently a memorial column to those who had fallen was erected at Calcutta.

On the 19th January 1844, terms of peace having been arranged, the young Rajah of Gwalior was installed upon his throne by the Governor-General. The following day the whole Army was reviewed and the orders issued for the return of the troops to their several cantonments. On the 3rd February the Corps reached Agra, and on the 19th was back in its own quarters at Bareilly. Major Cautley succeeded Major Oldfield in command of the Regiment, and he in turn was succeeded by Captain Hill the following year.

Whilst at Bareilly Mir Hidyat Ali got himself into serious trouble for sacrificing cows in the lines during the Bukir Eid, which led to a free fight between the Mohammedans and Hindoos of the Regiment. He took the whole blame upon himself in the most manly way, begging that the N.C.O.s and sowars concerned in the affair might be exonerated. He was removed from his appointment as Woordie Major, but upon Captain Hill's strong recommendation and in consideration of his former exemplary conduct the Commander-in-Chief was pleased to sanction his being restored to the appointment.

On the 25th November 1845 orders were unexpectedly received for the Regiment to march to the frontier, and to be prepared in every way for immediate active service. Trouble had for some time been brewing with the Sikhs, and culminated in the outbreak of the " First Sikh War " in December.

A wing of the Regiment was hurried forward by forced marches to join " The Army of the Sutlej," which had been assembled on the frontier and put in motion to resist the

Sikh invasion.   This detachment was present at the battles
of Mudki and Ferozeshahr on the 18th and 19th of
December.

The Regiment left Bareilly on the 1st December, arrived
at Meerut on the 12th, and here received orders to push
on at once to the frontier. Basseau was reached on the
1st January 1846, and Mudki, the scene of the first engagement, on the 4th. On the 7th January the Regiment
proceeded to take up an advanced position near the
bridge of boats, constructed by the enemy across the
Sutlej. Cavenagh writes :

" We reached our ground about one o'clock, and immediately pushed forward pickets in the direction of the river,
our furthermost post being close to a ruined mud tower
in the immediate vicinity of the bridge.   Here our patrols
met those of the 8th Regiment, which Corps held a position
about a mile to our left, though separated from our camp
by a deep ravine.   The main body of the Army was about
four miles in our rear, and we had no immediate supports.
It was, therefore, necessary to be at all times on the alert.
Our outposts and videttes extended for several miles,
and I personally visited them three times in the twenty-
four hours.   The greater part of my time, therefore,
was spent in the saddle.   In the daytime the old mud
tower above alluded to was a favourite place of resort,
as with the aid of a glass the Sikh camp and the movements
of the troops could be plainly perceived.   At times parties
used to cross the bridge and threaten our pickets, but no
serious attack was ever made, and our posts were never
driven in.   In one instance, however, the Sikhs were in
sufficient force to induce the officer commanding the
advanced post to send in a trooper to give the alarm.   As
he was seen galloping into the camp, the men seized their
arms and rushed to their horses, and in a few minutes
after the trumpet sounded, the Corps was mounted, the
tents struck, and the baggage packed in readiness for
despatch to the rear.   On two occasions whilst patrolling

in front of the videttes, I came upon some suspicious-looking Sikhs, whom I made prisoners and sent to headquarters. One morning a villager pointed out a Sikh trooper who, he said, belonged to a party that had crossed the river during the night in search of forage. After a sharp gallop I overtook the supposed Sikh, when, to my surprise, he turned round with a laugh, and I recognised one of my own men whom I had sent out in disguise to obtain intelligence. He had seen the Sikhs in the distance, and had intended following them into their camp, thinking that it might be supposed that he was a straggler from their party. I had charge of the intelligence department with our camp, and had no difficulty in obtaining, by means of my own, full information relative to the strength and position of the Sikh Army. They used to carry with them a store of parched peas, and when they came across a battery they took out the number corresponding with the number of guns and tied them up in a knot in their waist-cloth to serve as an *aide memoire*."

Information having been received that the enemy were threatening an attack on Ludhiana, Her Majesty's 16th Light Dragoons, the 3rd Light Cavalry, and 4th Irregular Cavalry were despatched to join Sir Harry Smith's Division for the relief of that station.

" We joined Sir Harry's force on the 20th at Jugraon, after two very long and fatiguing marches, the road being extremely heavy. The first day the march was twenty-five miles ; we did not reach our encamping ground before 3 p.m., and I was immediately required to put a strong picket of our men on the left flank of our position. The men had had nothing to eat, and the picket was placed on a sandy plain, without any shelter ; yet when I asked if there was anything I could procure for them, they stated that all they required was water for their horses, as without the means of quenching their thirst they would become unfit for work. Nothing was said with regard to their own wants.

" The force moved from its ground at one a.m. on the 21st, the Cavalry Brigade and Horse Artillery leading ; the four Infantry Regiments and Light Field Battery in the rear. Owing to a wheel having come in contact with a stump of a tree whilst passing through a village, one of the guns had to be halted for repairs. This caused a stoppage of the whole of the rear of the column. When the accident had been remedied, the mounted portion proceeded at a smart trot to overtake their Brigade. Thus there was an interval of about a mile between the rear Corps of Cavalry and the leading Regiment of Infantry.

"A little before sunrise a native brought to Captain Hill a letter addressed to the General from Colonel Godby, commanding at Ludhiana. The man stated that the enemy had moved from his entrenchments, and was about five miles from us, at a village called Budiwal, and that his force consisted of six Standards, or Corps, of Cavalry, and ten Regiments of Infantry, with forty-two guns. Captain Hill immediately conveyed the letter to the General, for which he was thanked ; but upon mentioning that the native who brought it would give information relative to the enemy's movements, he was desired to rejoin his Corps. Immediately afterwards Lieutenant Swetenham, of the 16th Lancers, escorted by twenty troopers of the Regiment, was ordered to proceed to Ludhiana with a despatch for Colonel Godby, directing him to move towards Budiwal to form a junction with the relieving force.

"Although we were close to the enemy, no steps were taken apparently to ascertain correctly his position, numbers, etc., and the interval between the Cavalry and Infantry still continued. The Sikhs were not so supine, for two Shutur sowars (camel riders) were at times observed on the left of our column, who were evidently watching our movements and who hurriedly rode off when they noticed that attention was drawn towards them.

" When within two miles of Budiwal the halt was sounded.

After about a quarter of an hour had elapsed we again advanced in the same order as before. We had not proceeded above a mile when the kettle drums of the Sikh Cavalry were heard on our left, and we soon perceived the whole of the Sikh Force marching out of some brushwood about half a mile distant. They then proceeded to take up a position on some sandhills parallel to the road along which we were moving, and about 500 yards from it, their left resting on a small village surrounded by a mud wall some ten feet in height. We steadily continued our route.

"At this time my first charger, which I had only mounted during the halt, became so restive that, after vainly trying to quiet him, I determined to remount my second charger, which, fortunately, was nigh at hand. Jumping off hastily, my wooden leg sank into the sand, and until one of my orderlies hastened to help me, I was in the unpleasant predicament of standing under a heavy fire between my two horses, and unable to mount either.

" In the meanwhile the Regiment had been drawn up in close columns of squadrons facing the Sikh Army, and within range of their guns. As the ground in front was not adapted for cavalry movements, we simply served as a target upon which the enemy might amuse themselves by practising until our tired Infantry came up from the rear. We soon had several casualties ; and then, in obedience to instructions from our Brigadier, who at once recognised the false position in which we had been placed, retired about 600 yards, and deployed on the third Squadron. During this manœuvre the men were unsteady; but with few exceptions our native officers became casualties and were sent to the rear, and the troopers had no one to look to for guidance. Under any circumstances, moreover, a retirement in column effected under a heavy artillery fire must be a nervous operation, especially with Cavalry. As soon, however, as our line was formed, and we again faced the danger, the unsteadiness ceased. In the meanwhile a mass of the enemy's Cavalry debouched from the rear of the village, with the view, apparently, of driving back the head of the column. Her Majesty's 16th Lancers immediately showed front to their assailants and prepared to attack by alternate squadrons. The Sikhs did not await to receive their charge, but at once retired upon their guns, suffering severe loss from our Horse Artillery.

" Whilst these operations were being carried on, our Infantry and Field Battery reached the scene of action, and passing along the front of our line proceeded in the direction of Ludhiana. They suffered severely from the enemy's fire ; but footsore and weary as they were, some of them having marched over fifty miles within little more than twenty-four hours, when our guns opened it seemed as if an electric shock had passed through their ranks. A hearty cheer pealed out, and every man drew himself up as erect as if he had only just come on parade. After they had passed, the order was given ' threes right,' and we continued our march. The Sikhs immediately took advantage of their front being clear to fling forward their right, pouring a very heavy artillery fire upon our retreating troops. At the same time a large body of their Cavalry commenced plundering our baggage, which extended for miles along the open country.

" Upon perceiving that our force made no preparations for the attack, the Sikh troops again pushed forward, threatening our rear and left flank. Our Cavalry accordingly a second time advanced to the charge, and our Infantry formed line to the left. Our Artillery opening upon our assailants, they rapidly retired, and our flank being thus cleared our line changed front left back to oppose the Sikh Infantry menacing our rear, and retired by alternate Regiments, Infantry and Artillery in the centre, and Cavalry on both flanks. The 4th Regiment of Irregular Cavalry were moving along some hard ground, and suffered from the ricochet shot. I had pointed out to my commanding officer that by taking ground to the left in some ploughed land we should escape the effects of this fire, and we had just completed the movement, I being the extreme right and still on the hard ground, when I was struck on the left arm by a ricochet ball—I believe the last that reached us. The Sikh troops evidently did not like to proceed far from their entrenchments, and their fire gradually ceased.

" When we had left Budiwal two miles in our rear, a very ominous cloud of dust appeared on the horizon, and at one time it was feared that we were about to be called upon to defend ourselves from a fresh body of assailants ; but after a short interval an advanced party in the French-grey uniform were seen emerging out of the dust, and the action was barely over when we were joined by the Ludhiana garrison, consisting of four guns Horse Artillery, one Regiment of Light Cavalry, and four Regiments of Native Infantry. Owing to the long marches, our men, and, as regards the Field Battery, horses, were dead beat, and we therefore continued our march. I remained on horseback until we arrived in sight of the cantonments, when riding up to a squadron of the 16th Lancers, drawn up on the left of the road along which the column was moving, in the hope of obtaining some water to quench my thirst, which, from the effect of my wound, was excessive, I suddenly became so faint that I could no longer sit in my saddle, and I was placed upon a horse-cloth which an officer kindly had spread on the ground for my use. Although no water was procurable, I obtained a little wine to moisten my parched lips, and after some delay a litter was brought, in which I was conveyed to the station."

The office and all Regimental records were lost this day when the enemy attacked and plundered the baggage. On the 27th January Sir Harry Smith moved out from Ludhiana and attacked the enemy at Aliwal. In his despatch to the Governor-General on the battle of Aliwal Sir Hugh Gough says :

" The 1st and 3rd Light Cavalry and the 4th Irregular

Cavalry, I believe, he has not seen in action, and it is my duty joyfully to report the manner in which they contended for the glorious prize of victory in the many charges they that day delivered."

In these charges on the Sikh squares Lieutenant Small Page, the Adjutant, two Dafadars, and four sowars were killed.

On the 10th February was fought the battle of Sobraon, which brought the war to a victorious conclusion. Under the treaty of peace the whole of the Jullundur Doab was ceded to the Company. The towns in the plains submitted without demur, but the " Kiladar " of Kot Kangra refused to surrender, and in April 1846 the Regiment joined a column under Brigadier Wheeler which was despatched for the subjugation of that place.

Twelve months batta was granted to all troops engaged in this campaign. The Regiment received permission to inscribe " Moodkee," " Ferozeshah," and "Aliwal " on its colours, and a medal was granted for each of the four great battles of the campaign.

Captain A. P. Martin and Lieutenant G. W. M. Hall joined the Regiment as Second in Command and Adjutant in 1846. The Regiment was quartered at Hoshiarpur for eight months, thence in 1847 it marched to Sullanpur and Benares. In 1849 it moved to Segowli and in 1851 to Jhansi. Captain Martin succeeded Major Hill in command of the Regiment, and Lieutenant John Smith joined as Adjutant, Lieutenant Hall becoming Second in Command.

In 1852 the robber stronghold of Khureechu was attacked and destroyed by a detachment of the Regiment and 55th Native Infantry. The ringleaders, Heera Singh and Bakht Singh, were killed and the Jhansi district freed from a formidable nest of outlaws.

In 1856 the Regiment moved to Hansi, and in this year Risaldar Mir Imam Bux received the 2nd Class of the Order of British India.

Extract from Bengal Army List " January 1857 "

4TH IRREGULAR CAVALRY

Hansi, arrived 6th February 1854.

Detachments at Hissar and Sirsa.

"Afghanistan " ; " Ghuznee " ; " Maharajpoor " ; 2 Rissalahs " Kelat " ;
Detachment " Moodkee " ; Detachment " Ferozeshuhur " ; "Alliwal."

Rank, Names and Corps.	Army Rank.	When Appointed.	Remarks.
Major A. Martin, 33rd N.I.	28 Nov.1854	18 Feb. 1846	Commandant, 23 Nov. 1850.
Captain G. W. M. Hall, 26th L.I.	12 June 1856	22 Feb. 1846	Second in Command, 23 Nov. 1850.
Lieutenant J. Smith, 44th N.I. . .	20 Aug. 1847	23 Nov. 1850	Adjutant.
Assistant Surgeon F. F. Allen . .	20 Nov. 1848	8 Dec. 1852	—
Ressaldar Meer Hydait Ally . .	—	26 Aug. 1853	Sirdar Bahadur.
Ressaldar Meer Emam Bux . . .	—	12 Sept.1856	Bahadur.

CHAPTER XIII

1857–1859

NEWS of the outbreak of the Mutiny at Meerut was brought to Major Martin at Hansi by a Mr. Metcalfe, who had with the greatest difficulty succeeded in escaping from Delhi. At this time one troop was at Hissar with a detachment at Sirsa, and a large number of men were away at their homes on furlough.

Finding himself isolated in the centre of the disaffected area, and placing no reliance on the Battalion of Hariana Infantry stationed at Hansi, Major Martin decided to call in his detachments and, leaving all baggage and convalescent men behind, to make a rapid march to Kurnal and join the Army assembling there under the Commander-in-Chief. The troop at Hissar rejoined, but the detachment at Sirsa was carried away with the tide of insurrection. Soon after the departure of the Regiment the Hariana Infantry mutinied, killed some of the British officers, and plundered and burnt the bungalows.

Many of the men on furlough were unable to rejoin the Regiment. Risaldar Mir Hidyat Ali, Sirdar Bahadur, was at his home at Mohna in the Gurgaon District, twenty-eight miles from Delhi. With him were his kinsmen Risaldar Ameer Ali and Kote Dafadar Waris Ali, both of the Regiment. A party of twenty-eight Europeans, military, civil, railway, and customs officials, employed with the Bhurtpore State, were endeavouring to make

their escape to Agra, when they were held up at the crossing of the Jumna at Mohna Ghat by insurgent sepoys
of the 9th Native Infantry and Oudh Cavalry. According to
an account given by one of the members of their party, Mr.
G. F. Harvey, Commissioner Agra Division, a trooper of the
12th Irregular Cavalry advised them to go to the village of
Risaldar Mir Hidyat Ali, where he assured them they would
be well received. Continuing his account, Mr. Harvey
says :

"We arrived at midday. The Risaldar supplied us
with everything in his power to bestow. I am sure that
his soldierly, hospitable welcome, and subsequent attention
to our comforts, during a stay of more than a week, will be
long remembered by all of us. During our stay some 300
of the 2nd Oude Cavalry in revolt, having murdered the
officers with them, Captain Fletcher, Hayes and Captain
Barber, etc., crossed the river and threatened to attack
us. Mir Hidyat Ali gave us warning, put on his uniform
and arms, called out his adherents, and assisted us in
making preparations to defend a chabutra in front of the
house ; and these timely preparations, together with the
fact that we had twenty-eight double-barrelled guns and
some dozen revolvers in the hands of Europeans, becoming
known to the scoundrels, they gave us a wide berth ; but
we were all impressed with the bearing and resolution
to aid us by the Risaldar.

"Some days later, having information that a party
was likely to be sent out for our destruction by the rebels
at Delhi, from which place we were only twenty-eight miles
distant, we determined not to place Hidyat Ali's family
at the mercy of the rebels by prolonging our stay with
him, and we made a night ride, escorted for some distance
by the Risaldar and his friends, across the country to
Sohana, where we fell in with the troops of the Maharajah
of Jeypur under Captain Eden, the Political Agent, with
whom I remained until the 20th July."

On arrival at Karnal, Captain Hall was sent off with a

troop to Meerut with despatches for General Wilson, and by marching night and day arrived there on the 26th May. From there he marched with the Meerut column to Delhi and was present at the battles on the Hindan on the 30th and 31st May. The Meerut column joined hands with the column from Karnal under the Commander-in-Chief at Alipore on the 7th June, and Hall's troop rejoined the Headquarters of the Regiment.

A detachment under the Adjutant, Lieutenant John Smith, had been sent to Mazaffarnagar to guard the Treasury. Here on the 21st June mutineers of the 5th Irregular Cavalry plundered the Treasury and Lieutenant John Smith was murdered. His grave is in the small churchyard at Mazaffarnagar.

On the 17th June Hall was sent to post a detachment of the Regiment at Lassowlie, on the line of communication to Ambala.

On the 19th June a sowar of the Regiment, Pir Khan, saved the life of General Hope Grant. The following account of this act of gallantry is taken from Sir Hope Grant's Memoirs :

"A sepoy within five yards of me fired at my horse, and put a bullet through his body, close to my leg. It was singular he did not aim at me ; but in all probability he thought it best to make sure of killing the horse, and that then, to a certainty, the rider would fall into his hands. I felt that my poor charger had received its death-wound ; yet he galloped on fifty yards through the throng of rebels, and then dropped down dead. I was in a rather awkward predicament—unhorsed, surrounded by the enemy, and, owing to the darkness, ignorant in which direction to proceed, when my orderly, a native sowar of the 4th Irregulars, by name Pir Khan, rode up to me, and said, ' Take my horse ; it is your only chance of safety.' I could not but admire his fine conduct. He was a Hindostanee Mussulman, and it would have been easy for him to have killed me and gone over to the enemy ; but he behaved nobly,

and was ready to save my life at the expense of his own.   I
refused his offer ; but, taking a firm grasp of his horse's
tail, I told Pir Khan to drag me out of the crowd.   This
he performed successfully with great courage.   I may
here mention that the next morning I called him into my
tent (he was a fine-looking fellow, of tall stature, about
twenty-five years of age), and after praising him for his
gallant behaviour, I offered him some little money ; upon
which he drew himself up with great dignity, salaamed,
and said, ' No, sahib, I will take no money ; but if you
will get my commanding officer to promote me, I shall
be very grateful.'   I answered him that I would make a
request to that effect, but urged him also to receive the
money. ¦He reluctantly took it and left the tent ; but
the next morning I received a note from his commanding
officer, Major Martin, returning the rupees, and stating
that Pir Khan could not be prevailed upon to accept them.
Major Martin promoted him ; and in consequence of my
favourable mention of him, Sir Henry Barnard awarded
him the 2nd Class Order of Merit."

Some years afterwards, when General Hope Grant was
commanding at Lucknow, he sent for Pir Khan and Kummoo Khan, who had on another occasion rendered him
conspicuous service, and presented them each with a
sword of honour.

The 9th and 17th Irregular Cavalry having been sent
off on distant duties, as they could no longer be relied on,
the Regiment was the only Hindustani Corps in the force
and was regarded with suspicion by the other units.   On
the 26th July the Regiment was disarmed and the men
given permission to return to their homes.   This was a
severe blow.   The men implored not to be sent away,
and permission was eventually obtained by Major Martin
for them to remain in the camp.   Here, unarmed, they
acted as police and performed their duties faithfully and
without a desertion, and on the fall of Delhi on the 11th
September their horses and arms were restored to them.

As General Hope Grant says in his Memoirs, " Every
precaution had to be taken," and he records a rather
touching incident of how when the Regiment was ordered
to lay down its arms, his two orderlies, Pir Khan and
Kummoo Khan, brought their swords to him instead of
laying them on the heap and said : " Sahib, take you our
swords and do not humble us so ; we have done nothing
to deserve it." " I felt it would be unjust to treat them
as disloyal subjects. I took their swords, and the next
day, with the approval of General Wilson, returned them
to their owners, giving them permission likewise to retain
their horses—a great boon to these fine fellows."

The Regimental banker, Pandit Pran Nath, was on
leave at his house in Delhi when the Mutiny broke out,
and could not rejoin. His family had been the Regimental
bankers ever since the Corps had been raised. His younger
brother, Pundit Janki Nath, was with the Regiment.
Pran Nath maintained constant secret correspondence
with Major Martin throughout the siege. Just before the
storming of Delhi Major Martin sent him a message to
remain in his house, and that he would come personally
with an escort and transport to bring him and his belong-
ings out of the city to the camp. On the day Major Martin
happened to be Field Officer on duty and was delayed, and
Pran Nath, fearing the fury of the mutineers in their
desperate flight from the city, unfortunately attempted
to rejoin the Regiment, and was shot as he tried to enter
the British camp.

The gallantry of Sowar (afterwards Risaldar) Chanda
Singh is worthy of record. A body of insurgents attempted
to force the bridge of boats across the Jumna to attack the
camp. Captain Hall with twenty men was sent to hold
them off. Hall called for a volunteer to cut the bridge.
Handing over his horse to another man, Chanda Singh
rushed forward under heavy fire to the centre of the
bridge and cut the cables with his sword. He received
three bullets through his clothes, but came out unharmed.

For this act of gallantry he received the 3rd Class Order of Merit. For his services before Delhi Captain Hall received the Brevet of Major.

Towards the end of September Captain Hall with two troops raised by Sirdar Salah Muhamed, and now incorporated with the Regiment, escorted the heavy guns of Colonel Greathead's column, which was despatched in pursuit of the rebels who had escaped from Delhi and were endeavouring to enter Oudh. The column arrived before Bulandshahr on the 28th, attacked and completely defeated a rebel force which attempted to cover that town, then pushed on, and occupied it and Malagarh. At Aligarh urgent appeals for assistance were received from Agra, and in response to these, Greathead hurried to its relief. Salah Muhamed was the Afghan Sirdar who had charge of the British prisoners from Kabul in 1842. He had brought them back safely from the Bamian, whither they had been sent by Akbar Khan on the approach of Pollok's Army. For his services he received a pension of one thousand rupees a month from the British Government and had settled in Ludhiana, as he was now an exile from Afghanistan. When the Mutiny broke out he volunteered his services. He joined as a Native Commandant on Rs.500 per month, with his younger brother Fateh Mohamed as Risaldar. He brought with him 120 to 130 men, of whom twenty were Kabulis, his relatives and personal servants, thirty Sikhs engaged at Ludhiana, and the remainder Punjabi Mohammedans. One of his adherents, Muhamed Kazim, who joined as a 2nd Jemadar, eventually became Risaldar Major of the Regiment. Another troop under the Adjutant, Sir Attock King Lake, Bart., was employed in the Gurgaon District.

In the absence of Major Martin, who had gone home on sick-leave, Brevet-Major Hall received orders in March 1858 to reconstruct the 4th Irregular Cavalry of Rajputs from the Hariana and Mynpuri Districts and Mussulmans from Delhi and Gurgaon. This he accomplished in about five months. It was difficult to obtain men who could bring their own horses. Horses had to be obtained for those who could not. From the Remount Agent 149 remounts were received and paid for by monthly instalments of Rs.5. Pundit Janki Nath, who had now become the Regimental banker in the place of his brother Pran Nath, raised the money to purchase the remainder. His bank had been almost ruined by the Mutiny, yet at great personal risk he made the effort and enabled Major Hall to complete the Regiment to establishment.

In October the Regiment marched to Cawnpur to take part in the operations that were being initiated for the reconquest of Oudh. The general plan was a big drive by a large number of columns which would force the rebels out of Oudh into the jungles of Nepal. These operations were under the personal direction of the Commander-in-Chief. On the 16th November the Regiment joined General Troupe's column. There is nothing of much interest to record in the operations of these various columns. On the 18th November the Regiment was present at the battle of Mehndi Ghat, and by the end of the year Oudh was cleared of the rebels. To prevent the return of the rebels who had fled before our columns into Nepal, a force was left under General Hope Grant to close the frontier. The Regiment remained in camp till July 1859 watching the banks of the Gogra, and then moved into quarters at Sitapur.

In August Major Hall was appointed Commandant, with Captain Ward as Second in Command, and Lieutenant Cadell, V.C., Adjutant, and Captain C. W. Crag, Duty Officer.

With the reconquest of Oudh the story of the war of the Indian Mutiny, so far as the Bengal Army is connected with it, comes to a close. The country had not been entirely cleared of the rebels and the Regiment was employed in Bundelkhand with small flying columns in hunting down and dispersing wandering bands. On conclusion of

8

these operations in the spring of 1860 the Regiment went into quarters at Nowgong.

In addition to the rewards for gallantry already mentioned, the following men of the Regiment received the 3rd Class Indian Order of Merit :

Risaldars Ahmed Syed Khan, Ghulam Nabi Khan, Muhamed Jaffar Khan, Jahangir Beg; Naib Risaldar Muhamed Kazim Khan ; Jemadars Ali Hussain, Rahim Bux Khan, Waris Ali, Wazir Ali, Auraf Ali ; Dafadars Data Ram, Nur Muhamed Khan, Kummoo Khan, Unwar Khan, Jehan Beg.

Risaldar Fateh Mohamed Khan received the 2nd Class Order of British India.   For his services in saving the lives of the party of Europeans, Risaldar Mir Hidyat Ali, Sirdar Bahadur, received a sword of honour, value Rs.1,000, and the Jagir of Mohna, worth Rs.5,000 a year.   His family still hold the Jagir, and it has been the custom of the head of the family to visit the Regiment whenever it is in the neighbourhood of Delhi, and bring with him this sword.   Mir Hidyat's family has served the Government of India for over a hundred years, and their loyalty has always been of the highest type, and deserves the most cordial recognition not only by the Government but by every British man and woman who is capable of gratitude.

Extract from the Bengal Army List " January 1863 "

3RD BENGAL CAVALRY

"Afghanistan " ; " Ghuznee " ; " Maharajpore " ; 2 Ressallahs " Kelat " ;
Detachment   " Moodkee " ; Detachment   " Ferozeshuhur " ; "Alliwal."
Late 4th Irregular Cavalry.
Headquarters at Bareilly—Arrived 5th December 1862.
Detachments at Moradabad and Futtehgurh.

Rank, Names and Corps.	Army Rank.	Appointment.	Remarks.
Major G. W. M. Hall, Staff Corps . .	19 Jan. 1858	22 Feb. 1846	Commandant, 26th Aug. 1859, Europe, M.C. for 20 months, from Officiating
Major W. R. E. Alexander, Staff Corps .	2 Mar. 1862	3 April 1862	Commandant.
Captain C. F. Packs, Staff Corps . .	18 Feb. 1861	5 Dec. 1859	Second in Command. Leave to Almorah, on P.A., to 15 Oct.
Lieutenant B. Cracroft, late 50th N.I. P.H.	21 Feb. 1857	15 June 1860	Adjutant, 6th March 1861.
Captain T. C. Graham, late 4th E.L.C. .	22 Sept.1861	28 Oct. 1862	—
Lieutenant A. Shepherd, late 5th En. L.C. . . .	9 Jan. 1857	29 Nov. 1862	Leave to Europe, for 1 year, on P.A., from 10th June 1863.
Lieutenant A.Murray, late 60th N.I.	30 April 1858	23 June 1860	Paid doing duty Officer, 23rd May 1863, Europe, M.C., for 20 months, from the 27th Mar. 1863.
Lieutenant J. R. Pearson, Staff Corps.	30 April 1858	17 May 1862	Paid doing duty Officer. Officiating Adjutant Lahore Light Horse.
Lieutenant G. W. Willock, General List, Cavalry .	21 Feb. 1861	18 Nov. 1862	—
Lieutenant E. H. Willock, General List, Cavalry .	1 Jan. 1862	9 Dec. 1862	—
Cornet S. A. Swinley, General List.	20 April 1861	10 Nov. 1862	On leave, at Nynee Tal.
Surgeon J. S. Morrieson, M.D. .	7 Aug. 1857	5 Feb. 1862	

CHAPTER XIV

1860–1880

FOR the next twenty years the Regiment saw no active
service. It was a period of reorganisation following on
the storm and confusion occasioned by the outbreak of
the Mutiny. On the 9th September 1859 an order had
been published detailing the Regiments and parts of
Regiments which had shown themselves " proof against
temptation, fanaticism, and threats," and mentioning the
special services of all such Corps. The order concluded
by enumerating the Regiments which would thence-
forward cease to exist in the Bengal Army. In May
1861 orders were issued for the reorganisation of the
Cavalry, the Regiment becoming the 3rd Bengal Cavalry.
The old yellow uniform was given up and replaced by red,
British officers were placed in command of squadrons,
and the organisation and command of the Regiment made
to conform more closely to that of the Regular Army. In
1862 the Regiment moved from Karnal to Bareilly.

In 1864 the composition of the Regiment was again
changed to one troop each of Mussalmans, Dogras, Sikhs,
Jats, Rajputs, and Brahmans.

From Bareilly the Regiment marched in January 1866
to Peshawar, from whence it moved on 3rd December 1868
to Jhelum, remaining there till 15th November 1871.
Risaldar Sheikh Nur Bux received the 1st Class Order of
British India.

In 1872 the Regiment attended the Camp of Exercise
held at Delhi, and then marched to Nowgong, where it

remained till the end of 1875. It was then ordered to Cawnpore, as escort to H.R.H. the Prince of Wales, and on completion of this duty marched in relief to Lucknow.

On the 21st July Colonel G. W. M. Hall, C.B., died at Nowgong. Colonel Hall must always be regarded as the foster-father of the Regiment. He was one of those men whose sterling worth the crisis of the Mutiny revealed. A born leader of men, it was his personality that carried the Regiment through the uncertain months of 1857. Succeeding Major Martin in 1858, he commanded the Regiment for nearly eighteen years. He was succeeded by Lieutenant-Colonel Brownlow, 7th Bengal Cavalry.

In 1878 Major A. R. D. Mackenzie was appointed to the command of the Regiment. He had joined the Regiment on its reorganisation in 1862. In May 1857 Mackenzie was at Meerut with his Regiment, the 3rd Light Cavalry, which was the first unit to break out into open revolt.

For anyone who had the privilege of knowing Sir Alfred Mackenzie (as he afterwards became), it is easy to understand how a man of his striking personality was able to retain a hold over some men in his squadron, when the remainder of the Regiment had mutinied. With his band of twenty-five men he rescued many isolated Europeans in the Meerut District. Everyone has heard of Hodson's famous ride with despatches from Ambala to Meerut, but few have heard how he was anticipated by Lieutenant Mackenzie. General Hewitt was anxious to get in touch with the Commander-in-Chief at Ambala, and Lieutenant Sanford volunteered to carry despatches to him. His offer was accepted, and Sanford then went to Mackenzie and asked him to escort him with his loyal men. This is not the place to record the perils of this ride ; it is sufficient to say that the party passed Hodson not far from Ambala.

In the autumn of 1878 the second Afghan War broke out. On the 21st October thirty sabres under Jemadar Mohamed Akram Khan left Lucknow for service with the Transport in Afghanistan. In January 1879 the

Regiment left Lucknow in four trains and arrived at Lahore on the 2nd February.   From Lahore the Regiment was railed to Jhelum and marched for Peshawar on the 3rd March.   A wing of the Regiment went to Hoti Mardan, and the Headquarters reached Peshawar on the 16th March and provided the posts of Shabkadir and Michni. The Treaty of Gandamak was signed and peace declared on the 6th June, the wing from Hoti Mardan rejoining the Regiment.   On the 3rd September 1879 the British Envoy at Kabul and his escort were massacred, and hostilities broke out afresh against Afghanistan.

The plan of campaign was for an advance to be made on Kabul by the force in the Kurram Valley under the command of Sir Frederick Roberts, and to support this, advance depôts were to be established on the Khyber route.

The Regiment was detailed to join the 2nd Brigade under Brigadier-General Arbuthnot to be established at Jalalabad. On the 27th September three troops under Major Cracroft proceeded to Jamrud, the Headquarters of the Regiment marching on the 3rd October.   On the 10th October Roberts entered Kabul.   On the 21st October a wing of the Regiment under Major Cracroft proceeded to Burikab, Headquarters to Jalalabad.

In December the situation at Kabul became critical, and on the 18th December Roberts was forced to entrench himself in the Sherpur Cantonments.   Troops on the Khyber route were hastened forward to his relief ; and on the 24th December Gough's Brigade reached Kabul.   The tribesmen on the Khyber route were quick to take advantage of our difficulties and harassed the advancing troops. Punitive expeditions against them became necessary to restore order.   On the 29th December a column under Lieutenant-Colonel Mackenzie, consisting of one troop of the Carabiniers, three troops 3rd Bengal Cavalry, two guns C.3 Royal Artillery, two Companies 1/12th Foot, 70 Rifles 27th Punjabis Infantry, set out from Jalalabad to Barikab, whence on the 30th it marched through Shershai against a cluster of villages in the heart of the Shinowri country, which were supposed to be sheltering some of the perpetrators of an outrage on the line of communication near Ali Boghan on the 24th. A night march was made followed by a surprise at dawn, and the enemy were completely surrounded. The plan was well conceived and skilfully executed, the force was thanked in Divisional Orders, and the Viceroy wired his congratulations.

The new year opened quietly in and around Kabul, where the principal interest of the moment was centred in the political question of the government of Afghanistan. On the 29th January 1880 the Regiment left Jalalabad and arrived at Sufaid Sung on 31st January. On the 8th February four troops, under Major Willock, marched towards Bordkhak, the intervening posts beyond Forte Battye being occupied by detachments from the Regiment. On 18th February the Headquarters marched to Kabul, arriving there on the 20th.

In March the Kabul Field Force was reorganised. Some of the troops on the Khyber line replaced worn-out Corps of the Kabul Force. The Regiment replaced the 5th Punjab Cavalry and marched out of Sherpur to join the Cavalry Brigade under Brigadier-General Gough, V.C., C.B.

On the 29th March the Ghazni Field Force, that is, the troops under Sir Donald Stewart's command, left Kandahar on the march for Kabul, and on the 16th April the 2nd Division under Major-General Ross, C.B., and the Cavalry Brigade, consisting of one Squadron 9th Lancers, the 3rd Bengal Cavalry, and the 3rd Punjab Cavalry under the command of Lieutenant-Colonel A. R. D. Mackenzie, marched from Kabul towards Ghazni to meet them. On the 19th April Sir Donald fought the battle of Ahmad Khel, twenty-three miles south of Ghazni, and on the 25th Mackenzie's Cavalry Brigade got in communication with him at Shashgao, Major-General Ross's Division being then at Saiadabad. The Ghazni Field Force marched on into the Logar Valley, where it became the 3rd Division of the Kabul Field Force, Sir Donald Stewart taking over supreme command from Sir Frederick Roberts.

During April, May, and June detachments and squadrons from the Regiment were engaged in various affairs against hostile gatherings and on escort duty. The Regiment formed part of the escort of the Chief Political officer, Sir Lepel Griffin, at the first interview with Abdul Rahman, the Amir-elect, which took place near Ak Sarai, sixteen miles north of Kabul, on the 31st July.

The news of the disastrous defeat of General Burrow's Brigade at Maiwand, and of the withdrawal of the Kandahar Force within the walls of that city, reached Kabul on the 28th July.

The object of the campaign had been attained, a friendly Amir placed on the throne, and the arrangements for the withdrawal of the Army from Afghanistan had been completed. The troops at Kabul were war-weary and were eagerly looking forward to the return to India. The situation in Southern Afghanistan was, however, critical, and Sir Donald Stewart determined to despatch a division from Kabul under Sir Frederick Roberts for the relief of Kandahar.

This decision to march a force through a hostile country without a base of operations or communications of any kind, towards a point presumably in the possession of the enemy, who had recently been successful, was condemned in no measured terms by many military critics. The result, however, justified the decision, and the march from Kabul to Kandahar has been recognised as a great military achievement.

The composition of the force which was finally selected to accompany Lord Roberts on his famous march will always be of interest to members of the Regiment.

Commanding: Lieutenant-General Sir Frederick Roberts, V.C.

Chief Staff Officer: Lieutenant-Colonel E. F. Chapman, R.A.

Cavalry Brigade: Brigadier-General Hugh Gough, V.C., C.B.

> 9th Lancers.
> 3rd Bengal Cavalry.
> 3rd Punjab Cavalry.
> Central India Horse.

Artillery: Colonel A. Johnson.

> 6/8th R.A. Mountain Battery.
> 11/9th R.A. Mountain Battery.
> No. 2 (Derajat) Mountain Battery.

2nd Infantry Division: Major-General Ross, C.B.

1st Infantry Brigade: Brigadier-General H. Macpherson, V.C., C.B.

> 92nd Highlanders.
> 23rd Pioneers.
> 24th Punjab Infantry.
> 2nd Gurkhas.

2nd Infantry Brigade: Brigadier-General T. B. Baker, C.B.

> 72nd Highlanders.
> 2nd Sikh Infantry.
> 3rd Sikh Infantry.
> 5th Gurkhas.

3rd Infantry Brigade: Brigadier-General C. M. MacGregor, C.B., C.S.I., C.I.E.

> 2/60th Rifles.
> 15th Sikhs.
> 4th Gurkhas.
> 25th Punjab Infantry.

Baggage had to be cut down to a minimum and the force had to subsist for the main part on the country. Long stretches of desert had often to be traversed without a drop

Extract from the Bengal Army List " July 1879 "

3RD BENGAL CAVALRY

Late 4th Irregular Cavalry (2nd Regiment Skinner's Horse)

Raised 6th December 1814

"Afghanistan"; "Ghuznee"; "Maharajpore"; "Kelat"; "Moodkee"; "Ferozeshuhur"; "Alliwal."

PESHAWAR.—Arrived 18th March 1879 from Lucknow.

Date of First Commission.	Rank, Names and Corps.	Army Rank.	First Appointment to Regiment.	Present Appointment in Regiment.	Remarks.
	COMMANDANT.				
30 Dec. 1854	Lieutenant-Colonel A. R. D. Mackenzie, I.E.L.C. . . . P.H.	23 July 1878	25 July 1863	17 Jan. 1878	—
	SQUADRON COMMANDERS.				
15 May 1854	Major B. Cracroft, S.C. . . . P.H.	15 May 1874	15 June 1860	17 Jan. 1878	Second in Command. Officiating Second Assistant Secretary to Government of Indian Military Department.
20 Jan. 1857	Major G. L. K. Hewett, S.C. . . P.H.	20 Jan. 1877	17 Jan. 1878	17 Jan. 1878	Furlough, m.c., 36 months, 18 Dec. 1876.
20 Oct. 1859	Captain G. W. Willock, General List Cavalry. . . . P.H.	20 Oct. 1871	18 Nov. 1862	17 Nov. 1875	Garrison Instructor, Coonoor.
	SQUADRON OFFICERS.				
9 Jan. 1863	Captain G. T. Morris, p.s., S.C. . H.S.	8 Mar. 1875	18 Dec. 1867	6 Mar. 1874	Adjutant, furlough, m.c., 2 years, 8 Oct. 1877.
13 July 1867	Lieutenant G. H. Elliott, S.C. . H.S.	17 Jan. 1870	18 July 1871	27 May 1872	Officiating Adjutant.
17 Nov. 1869	Lieutenant C. H. V. Garbett, S.C. . H.S.	28 Oct. 1871	6 Mar. 1874	6 Mar. 1874	Officiating Squadron Commander.
8 July 1869	Lieutenant H. N. Webb, S.C. . H.S.	28 Oct. 1871	13 Aug. 1877	13 Aug. 1877	—
	MEDICAL OFFICER.				
30 Mar. 1872	Surgeon E. Palmer . . . L.S.	30 Mar. 1872	1 Feb. 1879	20 Apl. 1879	—
	ATTACHED.				
20 Jan. 1860	Captain M. H. Court, G.L., Cavalry, H.S.-H.S.P.	20 Jan. 1872	24 Oct. 1878	24 Oct. 1878	—

NATIVE OFFICERS

Date of Entering Service.	Names.	Dates of Commission as			Remarks.
		Jemadar.	Ressaidar.	Ressaldar.	
	RESSALDARS.				
19 May 1857	Mahmed Kazim Khan	19 May 1857	1 May 1860	1 May 1863	Ressaldar Major, 1 Dec. 1871. Order of Merit, 3rd Class.
1 Jan. 1840	Ausuf Ally, Sardar Bahadur	24 May 1858	1 May 1865	1 Dec. 1871	Order of Merit, 3rd Class.
22 Oct. 1844	Burkut Ally	4 Apl. 1860	1 May 1868	1 May 1873	—
	RESSAIDARS.				
1 May 1852	Wajud Ally	4 Apl. 1860	1 May 1869	—	Woordie Major.
23 May 1864	Chunda Singh	26 July 1874	16 Sept.1876	—	—
14 June 1841	Jehan Beg	1 May 1865	15 Aug. 1877	—	Order of Merit, 3rd Class.
13 Sept. 1858	Mullock Singh	1 May 1876	1 Aug. 1878	—	—
	JEMADARS.				
15 Nov. 1848	Sheikh Shahamut	1 May 1876	—	—	—
1 May 1873	Mungul Singh	16 Sept.1876	—	—	—
12 June 1862	Mahomed Ukrum	15 Aug. 1877	—	—	—
1 May 1852	Ramjus Singh	1 May 1878	—	—	—
1 Oct. 1856	Umjud Ally	1 May 1878	—	—	—
16 June 1866	Dalmore Singh	1 Aug. 1878	—	—	—

Uniform : Drab. Facings : Blue. Lace : Gold. Armament : Snider Carbines and Pistols.

of water, causing great inconvenience and suffering to man and beast marching under a burning sun.

On Sunday the 8th August the march began. Ghazni was reached on the 15th, 139 miles in seven days. On the 16th the force marched to Ergatta, twenty miles. The Cavalry Brigade, which throughout the march performed the entire duties of advance guard, started at 4.30 a.m., but the rear guard did not reach camp till 9 p.m. The baggage animals were now beginning to show signs of distress, and as no local supplies were forthcoming at this stage, many animals remained unfed.

The next day, the 17th, Chardeh was reached, and here a message was received from the Officer Commanding at Kalat-i-Ghilzai giving news to the effect that Kandahar was closely invested. Kalat-i-Ghilzai was reached on the 23rd August, 225 miles in fifteen days.

The progress of the Force had been so satisfactory up to this point that Sir Frederick Roberts, having received reassuring reports from Kandahar, determined to rest his Division by halting at Kalat-i-Ghilzai over the 24th August.

On the 25th August the march was resumed. On the 26th a message was received at Tirandaz from Kandahar that the siege had been raised on the 23rd, and that on the morning of the 24th Sirdar Ayub Khan had struck his camp and retired to Mazra over the Baba Wali Kotal in the Arghandab Valley, where he was said to be entrenching.

On the 27th the Regiment and the 3rd Punjab Cavalry, under Brigadier-General Gough, starting at 1 a.m., made a double march of twenty-four miles to Robat, and succeeded in establishing heliographic communication with Kandahar.

From information received at Robat, from Kandahar, and from what General Roberts heard from other sources, he was led to believe that Ayub Khan intended to make a stand and was strengthening his position, which was said to extend from Gundigan to Kotal-i-Murcha.

On receipt of this news it was decided to make a halt at Robat on the 29th August to rest both men and animals, and to divide the remaining distance to Kandahar (nineteen miles) into two short marches, in order that the Force might arrive there fresh and fit for action.

With the arrival at Robat the suspense and strain of the forced marches were at an end. Since leaving Kabul the Force had covered 280 miles in twenty days or nineteen marches.

On the 30th August General Roberts's force marched seven and a half miles to Mohmand; and the next morning, at 3.30, it started on the remaining twelve miles to Kandahar. The advanced guard was composed of the 3rd Bengal Cavalry, two guns of C.2 Royal Artillery, and the 92nd Highlanders, and preparations were made to meet possible opposition in the neighbourhood of the city, before a position could be occupied for the camp.

Immediately after the camp had been established, General Roberts decided to carry out a personal reconnaissance of the covering position, and at 1 p.m., accompanied by his Chief Staff Officers, moved out with the following force under the command of Brigadier-General Gough :

> 3rd Bengal Cavalry.
> 15th Sikhs.
> 11/9th R.A. (2 guns).

The Infantry halted on the high ground above the villages of Gundizan and Murghan, and the Regiment, advancing another two and a half miles through difficult and enclosed country, beat up the enemy's position from flank to flank.

The enemy's Infantry hurriedly fell in and his batteries opened fire. Having completed his reconnaissance, the General ordered the Regiment to withdraw, which it did at the walk under Artillery fire. This reconnaissance was published in G.R.O.s, and Lieutenant-Colonel

Mackenzie was complimented on his handling of the Regiment.

As a result of his reconnaissance, General Roberts was able to form his plan of attack. Ayub's position was found to be too strong to be carried by a direct assault, and a turning movement was decided on.

On the next day, the 1st September, the enemy were attacked. The Cavalry Brigade was ordered to operate on the left flank, where it could best threaten the enemy's line of retreat.

The Infantry assault was successful, and the enemy out-manœuvred and driven from his position. The Cavalry Brigade advanced rapidly, scouting as far as Kohkaran, and there proceeded to execute the extended turning movement entrusted to it. The nature of the ground, however, necessarily precluded very direct or rapid progress, while the enemy's retreat, as soon as the Pir Paimal position was turned, was precipitate. Thus though the Brigade crossed the Aghandab, and pushed beyond the line of the enemy's retreat towards Khakrez, no regular troops were encountered, but some 350 of the fugitive tribesmen were killed.

This successful battle terminated the second Afghan War.

The Regiment commenced its return march to India on the 15th September, sharing en route in the operations against the Achakzais under Brigadier-General Baker, and reached Mian Mir on the 14th October 1880.

For their services in this campaign, Colonel Mackenzie was appointed Honorary A.D.C. to the Viceroy, Captain G. H. Elliot received the Brevet of Major, and Risaldar Major Muhamed Kazim Khan the 2nd Class Order of British India, subsequently being promoted to the 1st Class.

CHAPTER XV

1881-1899

TIRAH CAMPAIGN—SARAGARHI

ANOTHER long period of peace succeeded the second Afghan War.

In February 1884 the Regiment moved to Sialkot, and took part in the concentration of troops at Rawal Pindi for the reception of H.H. Abdur Rahman, Amir of Afghanistan.

In 1885 the Regiment took part in the Camp of Exercise held at Ambala. A squadron of Sikhs was added to the Regiment in this year. The next year, 1886, it moved to Loralai, which was reached on the 3rd January 1887.

On the 21st January 1887, Colonel A. R. D. Mackenzie, C.B., handed over command of the Regiment to Lieutenant-Colonel G. W. Willock. Colonel Mackenzie, on retiring, settled at Simla and Mashobra, where he lived to a great age. He received the K.C.B., and had the distinction of leading the Mutiny Veterans at the Delhi Durbar of 1903. Deafness, from which he suffered considerably during his latter years, prevented this distinguished soldier from continuing his career and filling a higher command for which he was so undoubtedly fitted.

On the 19th January 1888 the Regiment left Loralai, and reached Cawnpore on the 27th April. In 1889 it took part in a large Cavalry concentration at Lucknow under General Luck, the Inspector-General of Cavalry. In 1890 the uniform was changed from drab to blue.

In 1891 Colonel E. A. Money, 2nd Punjab Cavalry, took over command of the Regiment from Colonel Willock, who proceeded home on a year's leave pending retirement.

On the 5th February 1892 the Regiment arrived at

Fyzabad, having taken part en route in a Camp of Exercise at Aligarh, when it was inspected by Lord Roberts, the Commander-in-Chief.

In 1894 the Regiment won the Commander-in-Chief's Prize for Musketry and the first and second prizes Lloyd Lindsay Competition at the B.P.R.A. Meeting at Meerut.

In August 1895 Lieutenant-Colonel Elliot succeeded Colonel Money in command.

In 1896 permission was received to arm the front rank with lances.   No change in uniform or designation was involved.   In the Long Distance Reconnaissance Competition, in which the Commander-in-Chief was especially interested, the Regiment was highly commended, " the best report was received from the 3rd Bengal Cavalry," and many prizes were also taken at the Military Tournament at Calcutta.   The same year in signalling the Regiment was first on the list of Indian Cavalry (Instructor, Captain W. E. A. Blakeney).

Risaldar Major Mangal Singh, Sirdar Bahadur, went with the Indian Contingent to England for the Diamond Jubilee celebrations.

On the 10th June 1897 the Political Officer in the Tochi was treacherously wounded at Datta Khel.   On the 26th July, without any warning, vast numbers of tribesmen attacked the Chakdara and Malakand Posts ; and on the 7th August the Hadda Mulla, descending the Gandab Valley, attacked the Shabkadar Post with a following of about 5,000 men.

The situation on the North-west Frontier appeared so menacing that it was decided to concentrate at Rawal Pindi a 2nd and 3rd Reserve Brigade.   On the 14th August the Regiment received a telegram ordering it to proceed to Rawal Pindi to join the latter Brigade, to which it would be attached.

At this time of the year fully half the men of the Regiment were away at their homes on leave and furlough, the latter also having their horses with them.   On the

17th August the first troop train left Fyzabad, and by dint of exertion on the part of the Indian officers the furlough men with their horses were able to join the Regiment at Ambala as it passed through.

By the 24th August the Regiment was concentrated at Pindi, the day after the Khyber Posts were attacked.

On the 27th August sudden orders were received to proceed to Kohat, the activities of the Orakzai against the Samana Post necessitating the immediate reinforcement of the Kohat Garrison. The Kohat Kurram Force, as the troops detailed for this purpose were known, were placed under the command of Brigadier-General Yeatman Biggs and formed into two Brigades, the Regiment being attached to the 2nd Brigade.

On the 29th August the Regiment arrived at Kohat, having been railed as far as Khushalgarh. On the 31st August Major Middleton assumed command, Colonel Elliot having been evacuated sick, and on the 1st September the Regiment marched to Hangu. On the 12th September the 18th Royal Irish and the 3rd Gurkhas had just come down from the Samana, when an urgent message came in that Fort Gulistan was hard pressed. The signallers of the Regiment galloped out and got a message through Saragarhi that the Infantry Brigade would be up next day. Saragarhi was a small signalling post by which communication was maintained between Fort Gulistan and Fort Lockhart. Its garrison consisted of twenty-one men of the 36th Sikhs. That night Saragarhi was attacked. After a most gallant defence, in which the whole of the garrison perished, the post fell, not, however, before they had inflicted a loss of 180 killed on the enemy. The defence of Saragarhi is rightly considered one of the most illustrious feats of valour in the annals of the Sikhs.

In the meantime, the Regiment and four guns of No. 9 Field Battery, under Major Middleton, had moved out of camp, and, having been joined by two more guns from

9

Extract from the Bengal Army List "July 1897"

3RD REGIMENT OF BENGAL CAVALRY (LATE 4TH IRREGULAR CAVALRY)
(2ND REGIMENT SKINNER'S HORSE)

Raised in 1814.

CLASS SQUADRON REGIMENT.—1 Squadron Sikhs, 1 Squadron Jats, 1 Squadron Rangurs, ½ Squadron Rajputs, ½ Squadron Hindustani Mahomedans.

"Afghanistan"; "Ghuznee"; "Maharajpore"; "Kelat"; "Moodkee"; "Ferozeshuhur"; "Aliwal."
"Kandahar, 1800"; "Afghanistan, 1879-80."
Uniform: Blue. Facings: Yellow.

FYZABAD.—Arrived 5th February, 1892 from Cawnpore. (Under orders to Lucknow.)

Date of First Commission.	Rank, Names and Corps.	Army Rank.	First Appointment to Regiment.	Present Appointment in Regiment.	Remarks.
	COMMANDANT.				
13 July 1867	Lieutenant-Colonel G. H. Elliot (p.s.)	13 July 1893	18 July 1871	16 Aug. 1895	—
	SQUADRON COMMANDERS.				
28 Oct. 1876	Major H. J. J. Middleton (p.s.)	28 Oct. 1896	11 May 1883	1 Nov. 1888	Second in Command, 16 Aug. 1895.
30 Jan. 1878	Captain A. N. Carr (p.s.)	30 Jan. 1889	22 Dec. 1883	1 Nov. 1888	—
11 Aug. 1880	Captain C. Jackson (p.s.p.)	11 Aug. 1891	31 Aug. 1882	1 July 1892	—
10 May 1882	Captain W. E. A. Blakeney (s.p.)	10 May 1893	15 Feb. 1887	16 Aug. 1895	Leave out of India, p.a., 1 year, B.C.O., 28 July 1896.
	SQUADRON OFFICERS.				
10 May 1882	Captain C. L. Hamilton (p.s.)	10 May 1893	12 Aug. 1889	12 Aug. 1889	—
7 Feb. 1885	Captain F. L. Moore (p.s.)	7 Feb. 1896	24 Apl. 1897	6 July 1899	—
30 Jan. 1889	Lieutenant R. L. Morris	31 July 1891	4 Oct. 1892	16 Aug. 1895	Adjutant, 23 Apl. 1896. Leave out of India, m.c., 6 months, 1 June 1897.
3 Dec. 1890	Lieutenant A. Le F. Smith	24 May 1892	30 Oct. 1896	30 Oct. 1896	—
	MEDICAL OFFICER.				
30 Sept. 1886	Surgeon-Captain F. Thomson Wyville, M.B., C.M.	30 Sept. 1886	26 Sept. 1893	26 Sept. 1893	Officiating Medical Officer, Lawrence, Mly., Asylum, Sanawar.

	ATTACHED.				Remarks.
21 Jan. 1893	Lieutenant E. C. Loch	21 Apl. 1895	23 Nov. 1895	23 Nov. 1895	Officiating Squadron Officer. Leave out of India, p.a., 1 year, B.C.O., 20 Feb. 1897.
16 Jan. 1895	Lieutenant E. C. W. Conway-Gordon	16 Apl. 1897	19 Apl. 1896	19 Apl. 1896	Officiating Squadron Officer.
27 July 1892	Surgeon-Captain H. A. Smith, M.B., B.S. (Medical Officer, 11 B.I.).	27 July 1895	2 Jan. 1897	2 Jan. 1897	Officiating Medical Charge.

NATIVE OFFICERS

Date of Entering Service.	Names.	Jemadar.	Date of Commission as		Remarks.
			Ressaidar.	Risaldar.	
	RISALDAR MAJOR.				
1 May 1873	Mangal Singh	16 Sept. 1876	16 May 1881	5 Feb. 1888	Risaldar Major, 15 May 1894.
	RISALDARS.				
1 Nov. 1867	Ghulam Hasen Khan	4 June 1879	18 Sept. 1885	17 Aug. 1890	—
3 Jan. 1868	Farzand Ali (5)	8 Mar. 1880	8 Sept. 1885	11 Nov. 1890	—
22 Oct. 1872	Gurdatt Singh	16 Oct. 1889	14 Jan. 1890	4 Sept. 1896	
	RESSAIDARS.				
1 May 1874	Mohar Singh (14) (15)	29 June 1885	24 Oct. 1890	—	—
6 Nov. 1882	Jaswant Singh	29 Sept. 1888	11 Nov. 1890	—	Woordie Major, 15 May 1894.
1 June 1875	Hazwant Singh (14)	1 Jan. 1889	15 May 1894	—	—
	JEMADARS.				
23 Oct. 1871	Alamdar Husain	9 July 1887	1 Jan. 1896	—	—
1 July 1882	Ratan Singh (16)	9 July 1887	4 Sept. 1896	—	—
1 May 1874	Khubi Singh	11 Nov. 1890	—	—	—
1 Jan. 1879	Gulab Singh	15 May 1894	—	—	—
8 Feb. 1876	Gurdatt Singh	1 May 1895	—	—	—
1 May 1881	Lal Singh (14)	8 Dec. 1895	—	—	—
4 Jan. 1882	Haidar Shah (14)	1 Jan. 1896	—	—	—
9 July 1882	Jan Muhammad Khan	1 Jan. 1896	—	—	—
1 Feb. 1879	Harnarayan Singh	4 Sept. 1896	—	—	—

Doaba, occupied a position on the Foot Hills from which the guns could shell the tribesmen who were collecting for an assault on Fort Gulistan.

This action of the 3rd Bengal Cavalry and the 9th Field Battery, R.F.A., undoubtedly saved Fort Gulistan from a serious and resolute attack by the Orakzai Afridis, rendered savage as they were by the execution wrought on them by the detachment of the 36th Sikhs at Saragarhi. The next morning the 18th Royal Irish and the 3rd Gurkhas and the mountain guns got up to the relief of Gulistan. At the first sound of the guns the enemy dispersed and fled. The Regiment returned to Hangu late on the night of the 14th. During those two days and a half both men and officers subsisted on the emergency ration of parched gram.

On the 17th September the Regiment was ordered to Thull, and on the 20th September marched to Shinowari under sealed orders. The intention was that the Regiment should cross over the Chagru Kotal and make a raid down the Khanki Valley in conjunction with the 6th Bengal Cavalry from Usterzai, the Cavalry to be supported by strong Infantry columns on the Samana. This, at the last minute, must have been considered too hazardous an operation, as on the next day, the 21st September, the orders were countermanded.

On the 22nd September the Regiment was ordered to Sada to join Brigadier-General Richardson's Flying Column, and arrived there on the 27th.

On the 2nd October a patrol of the Regiment was ambushed and its leader, Dafadar Partap Singh, killed, and Sowar Maman Singh wounded. Sowars Diwan Singh and Sukhdeo Singh brought in their wounded comrade, and for their gallantry on this occasion were awarded the Order of Merit, third class.

On the 9th October the Regiment was ordered to join the Line of Communication Troops, Tirah Expeditionary Force, and was distributed as follows :

Headquarters and " C " Squadron at Shinowari.
" B " Squadron at Kai.
"A " Squadron at Hangu.
" D " Squadron at Usterzai.

On the 20th October the Tirah Expeditionary Force
under General Sir William Lockhart advanced from Shinowari, and on the same day was fought the battle of Dargai.

It is unnecessary here to record the operations of the
Tirah Expeditionary Force. By the middle of December
it had returned, having completed its task. Punitive
operations in the Bazaar Valley followed and the Khyber
had to be reoccupied, but by February 1898 the campaign
was at an end, On the 2nd February the Headquarters
and two Squadrons marched to Kohat, the remaining two
Squadrons being distributed between Usterzai, Hangu,
Kai, Thull, and Parachinar. The Regiment remained at
Kohat and in the Kurram till the 26th December 1898,
when it commenced its return march to Meerut, which was
reached on the 26th February 1899.

On the 30th September 1899, Colonel Elliott retired, and
was succeeded by Lieutenant-Colonel Middleton.

CHAPTER XVI

1901–1914

THE South African War began shortly after the conclusion of the Tirah Campaign, but unfortunately afforded the Regiment no opportunities for active service. A party of sixteen men, however, was sent out in 1902 under Risaldar Hanwant Singh for duty with Remounts.

Lieutenant C. L. Gaussen served with Damant's Horse, and was killed in action on the 24th December 1901. The column he was with had made a forced march on the night of the 23/24th December 1901, and at dawn came upon a much superior force of Boers at Tafel Kop. The Boers were dressed in khaki, and had got very close up before it was discovered who they were. In order to save the guns, Gaussen gave the order to charge. He was killed, and his Squadron suffered very heavy casualties. The charge, however, enabled the gunners to get their teams away, though they were forced to leave the guns. These the Boers were unable to move, and they were recaptured the next day when reinforcements arrived.

His younger brother, Lieutenant J. R. Gaussen, served with the 1st Skinner's Horse in China, and, as is recorded in the history of the 1st Corps, was awarded the D.S.O. for gallantry.

As far as can be ascertained, the Regiment commenced to play tournament polo in 1901. In that year the team consisting of Messrs. Stokes, Webber, Coaker, and Conway-Gordon was beaten in the Meerut autumn tournament by the 15th Hussars, who won the tournament. In the same month a team composed of Captain Gaussen, Mr.

Coaker, Risaldar Zalim Singh, and Mr. Conway-Gordon was beaten in the semi-final of the Cawnpore Challenge Cup by the 8th Bengal Lancers, who eventually won the final.

The Regiment was present at the Delhi Durbar of 1903, and a team was entered for the Durbar Polo Tournament, consisting of Mr. Vander Gucht 1, Mr. Coaker 2, Risaldar Zalim Singh 3, and Mr. Conway-Gordon, back. They were beaten by the 4th Poona Horse, the ultimate winners, in the second round. The same team, with the exception of Jemadar Malim Singh at 3, won the Dehra Dun Tournament in the same year.

In the Bengal Cavalry Tournament 1903, this team reached the semi-finals, being beaten by the 15th Bengal Lancers by 3 to 1.

In 1904, a team from the Regiment won the Naini Tal Tournament. Team: Mr. F. T. Vander Gucht 1, Mr. V. A. Coaker 2, Mr. E. C. W. Conway-Gordon back.

The same team with the addition of Major Hamilton then won the Dehra Dun Tournament of this year.

In November 1904 the Regiment marched in relief to Neemuch, where it arrived on the 25th December.

While on detachment with his Squadron at Nasirabad, Risaldar Thakur Zalim Singh was called out in aid of the civil power against a refractory chief. For his services on this occasion he was rewarded with the Indian Distinguished Service Medal. Thakur Zalim Singh commanded a half-Squadron of Jodpore Rajputs which had only recently been incorporated in the Regiment.

In February 1905 the Regiment marched to Sailana for the Mhow Division Manœuvres and was brigaded with the 10th Hussars, Central India Horse, and the Bhopal Imperial Service Lancers, under Colonel Dawson, Central India Horse.

In May 1905 Colonel Middleton was appointed A.A.G., Mhow, and was succeeded in command of the Regiment by Lieutenant-Colonel A. N. Carr.

Early in 1906 the Regiment again marched to Mhow for Divisional Training, taking part en route in a tactical exercise against a force of Cavalry from Mhow. During this exercise the Regiment covered a distance of 215 miles in seven days, only one horse and one mule going lame, although the route lay for the most part across difficult and rocky country—a really remarkable performance.

India at this time was experiencing one of its worst visitations of the plague ; the Regiment had to go out into a segregation camp in September 1906 and did not return to the lines till April of the following year.

Whilst the Regiment was practising swimming horses, Lance-Dafadar Harbhaj Singh (afterwards Risaldar) saved the life of Veterinary Assistant Muhammad Ahsan from drowning, and was awarded the Royal Humane Society's Medal. Muhammad Ahsan was crossing on a raft which sank, and getting entangled with a rope, was dragged to the bottom. Harbhaj Singh, seeing this, dived into the water, and was just able to cut the rope in time to save the man's life. A few years later Harbhaj Singh was again rewarded by the Royal Humane Society for saving the life of a blind child who had fallen down a well.

In January 1908 the Regiment won the Jodhpore Polo Tournament for which the team was Mr. Manderson 1, Mr. Coaker 2, Mr. Medlicott 3, and Captain Conway-Gordon back.

The same team represented the Regiment at the Bengal Cavalry Tournament in February, being beaten by the 18th Bengal Lancers.

In November Deo Singh 1, Mr. Manderson 2, Mr. Coaker 3, and Mr. Medlicott back, played in the Indore Tournament, and won the Rajputana and Central India Tournament in the following month.

In July 1908 Colonel A. N. Carr fell ill and was taken to hospital at Indore, where he died on the 30th September, deeply mourned by all ranks. His body was brought to

Neemuch for burial, and at their own special request, the Indian officers bore the coffin to the grave.

Lieutenant-Colonel W. E. A. Blakeney succeeded Colonel Carr in command of the Regiment.

In 1909 Risaldar Major Hanwant Singh received the second class Order of British India, afterwards being promoted to the first class. In this year he went to England as one of the Indian Orderly Officers to H.M. the King-Emperor.

In October the Regiment marched to Muttra for the Cavalry Division Manœuvres, held in the vicinity of Gurgaon, under the direction of Major-General Grover, the Inspector-General of Cavalry, and did not get back to Neemuch until March 1910.

In the following year the Regiment marched in relief to Meerut. Risaldar Ratan Singh received the second class Order of British India.

In December 1911 the Meerut Cavalry Brigade was at Delhi for his Majesty King George V's Durbar. The Military Review, when four Brigades of Cavalry and three Divisions of Infantry with detachments of Imperial Service Troops marched past His Majesty, was one of the finest displays of military force ever witnessed in India. A mixed Squadron under the command of Major Conway-Gordon had the honour of escorting their Majesties.

At the Indian Cavalry Polo Tournament at Ambala in February 1912 the Regimental team, after defeating the 9th Hodson Horse, 18th Lancers, and 4th Cavalry, were beaten in the final by the 17th Cavalry by 4 goals to 3. Team : Mr. Gray 1, Mr. Manderson 2, Captain Coaker 3, Captain Conway-Gordon back.

In the autumn of 1912 the Regiment took part in the Northern Army Manœuvres near Delhi under the direction of Lieutenant-General Sir James Wilcocks.

On the 23rd December 1912 the Regiment formed part of the escort to His Excellency the Viceroy, Lord Hardinge of Penshurst, on his first State visit to Delhi, as the Capital

of India.   As the procession was passing down the Chandi
Chauk, a bomb was thrown at His Excellency, who was
riding on an elephant with Lady Hardinge.   The two
attendants who were standing behind their Excellencies
were killed, the Viceroy was severely wounded, but
fortunately Lady Hardinge escaped unhurt.

In November the Regiment won the " Country Life "
Tournament at Allahabad, the team being Mr. Gray 1,
Captain Vander-Gucht 2, Captain Manderson 3, and Mr.
Lorimer back.

In the Indian Cavalry Polo Tournament, played at
Delhi in February 1913, the Regiment was beaten in the
semi-finals by the winners of the finals, the 17th Cavalry.
Team : Mr. Gray 1, Captain Vander-Gucht 2, Captain
Manderson 3, Major Conway-Gordon back.

In this year the Regiment won the British Officers'
Team Tent-pegging Trophy at the Indian Cavalry Tournament for the third year in succession.   The team on this
occasion consisted of Major J. R. Gaussen, Captain Conway-
Gordon, Captain Bennett, and Captain Manderson.

Colonel Blakeney completed his tenure of command in
September 1913, and was succeeded by Lieutenant-
Colonel E. W. Wall, of the 17th Cavalry.

The next year, 1914, the Regiment won the Dehra Dun
Polo Tournament, and were again in the final of Indian
Cavalry Tournament.   The team had the hard side of the
draw, and after knocking out such strong combinations
as the 39th Central India Horse, 23rd Cavalry, and 11th
Lancers, were beaten in the final by the 9th Hodson's
Horse by 4 goals to 2.   Team: Mr. G. C. G. Gray 1,
Captain G. T. Vander-Gucht 2, Captain R. W. Manderson
3, Mr. J. M. Lorimer back.

It was at pig-sticking, however, that the Regiment
gained such remarkable successes this year.   The Regimental team—Captain H. E. Medlicott, Captain R. W.
Manderson, Mr. G. C. G. Gray—won the Muttra Cup, a
team competition, killing six out of seven pig.

Captain H. E. Medlicott, who had in 1907 and 1909 won the Salmon and Guzerat Cups, won the Kadir Cup on " Drogheda."

Gray, in the following month, won both the Guzerat and Salmon Cups on " Sherdil " and " Joey " respectively.

The Regiment thus secured all the important pig-sticking trophies this year.

The year 1914 was the centenary of the 3rd Horse. Great preparations had been made for the centenary celebrations, which were to be held in December, but in August the Great War broke out, and the 7th December 1914 was spent at sea en route for France.

Risaldar Major Ashraf Ali Khan, who had been to England as one of the Indian Orderly Officers to His Majesty the King-Emperor, received this year the Order of British India, second class.

The composition of squadrons, and the squadron commanders, when the Great War broke out were :

" A " Squadron . . . Captain Medlicott
    Right Half . Rajputs of Eastern Punjab
    Left Half . Rajputana Rajputs, Jodhpore
" B " Squadron . . . Captain Hulbert
    Musalman Rajputs
" C " Squadron . . . Captain Vander Gucht
    Sikhs
" D " Squadron . . . Captain Coaker
    Jats

Extract from Indian Army List "July 1914"

3RD SKINNER'S HORSE

MEERUT.—Arrived 23rd November 1910 from Neemuch.

"Afghanistan"; "Ghuznee, 1839"; "Khelat"; "Maharajpore"; "Moodkee"; "Ferozeshah"; "Aliwal"; "Kandahar, 1880"; "Afghanistan, 1879–80"; "Punjab Frontier."

COMPOSITION.—1 Squadron of Sikhs, 1 of Jats, 1 of Rajputs, 1 of Musalman Rajputs. Uniform: Blue. Facings: Yellow.

First Command or Date of Entering Service.	Names and Rank.	Army Rank.	Present Appointment in Regiment.	Remarks.
	COMMANDANT.			
30 Jan. 1886	Lieutenant-Colonel E. W. Wall	30 Jan. 1912	1 Oct. 1913	—
	SQUADRON COMMANDERS (4)			
20 Feb. 1892	Major J. R. Gaussen, D.S.O. (Q)	20 Feb. 1910	9 Nov. 1913	Second in Command.
16 Jan. 1895	Major E. C. W. Conway-Gordon (p.s.c.)	16 Jan. 1913	1 Oct. 1908	Seconded.
28 Sept. 1895	Major C. E. Stokes (p.s.c.) L	28 Sept. 1913	2 July 1912	Seconded.
4 Aug. 1897	Captain M. R. H. Webber	4 Aug. 1906	15 Dec. 1912	Seconded.
	SQUADRON OFFICERS (9).			
22 Jan. 1898	Captain V. A. Coaker	22 Jan. 1907	12 Aug. 1900	—
20 July 1898	Captain G. T. Vander Gucht	20 July 1901	15 Sept.1901	—
24 Jan. 1900	Captain J. H. Bennett (L)	24 Jan. 1909	2 Aug. 1902	—
17 Feb. 1900	Captain T. E. Hulbert	17 Feb. 1909	26 Jan. 1903	—
2 May 1909	Captain H. E. Medlicott	2 May 1909	1 July 1907	—
22 Oct. 1902	Captain S. T. Polley	22 Oct. 1911	1 Nov. 1906	—
9 Jan. 1904	Captain R. W. Manderson	9 Jan. 1913	1 Sept. 1906	—
18 Jan. 1905	Captain A. M. Daniels	18 Jan. 1914	8 Jan. 1908	—
24 Jan. 1906	Lieutenant J. M. Lorimer	24 Apl. 1908	17 Sept.1909	Adjutant.
17 Aug. 1907	Lieutenant E. D. Metcalfe	17 Nov. 1909	14 Nov. 1909	Quartermaster.
9 Sept. 1908	Lieutenant G. C. G. Gray	9 Dec. 1909	26 Nov. 1909	—
5 Sept. 1911	Lieutenant B. Fitz H. Randall	5 Dec. 1914	3 Mar. 1914	—
	MEDICAL OFFICER.			
29 Jan. 1895	Major J. A. Hamilton, M.B., F.R.C.S.E.	29 July1906	25 Apl. 1900	—

NATIVE OFFICERS.

Date of Entering Service.	Names.	Date of Commissions as			Remarks.
		Jemadar.	Ressaidar.	Risaldar.	
	RISALDAR MAJOR.				
16 Sept. 1883	Ashraf Ali Khan, Bahadur (56)	18 Feb. 1896	1 Nov. 1899	16 Oct. 1905	Risaldar Major, 31 Aug. 1912. Order British India, 2nd Class.
	RISALDARS.				
1 Oct. 1894	Mir Shamshad Ali (56)	7 May 1899	1 Feb. 1901	16 Oct. 1910	—
21 Dec. 1891	Sheo Chand (56, 58)	21 May 1902	16 Oct. 1905	16 Mar. 1912	—
24 Sept. 1884	Balwant Singh	21 Dec. 1900	16 Oct. 1905	31 Aug. 1912	—
	RESSAIDARS.				
4 Apl. 1889	Sobha Singh (56, 62)	21 May 1902	1 Jan. 1906	—	—
16 Jan. 1894	Nur Muhammad Khan (56, 66)	1 Jan. 1905	16 Oct. 1910	—	—
8 Mar. 1902	Malan Singh	8 Mar. 1902	16 Mar. 1912	—	—
1 Jan. 1906	Mukand Singh (56)	1 Jan. 1906	31 Aug. 1912	—	—
	JEMADARS.				
26 June 1894	Wali Dad Khan (45a, 66)	1 Jan. 1907	—	—	Woordie Major, 1 Apl. 1913.
3 Jan. 1901	Raj Singh (45a, 56)	15 Feb. 1911	—	—	—
1 Oct. 1902	Channan Singh (45a)	15 Feb. 1911	—	—	—
3 Apl. 1888	Udai Singh (66)	16 Mar. 1912	—	—	—
4 Mar. 1896	Dhanwant Singh (66)	22 July 1912	—	—	—
1 Dec. 1901	Amar Singh	31 Aug. 1912	—	—	—
1 Aug. 1899	Harbhaj Singh (56)	1 Feb. 1913	—	—	—
8 Aug. 1900	Bhagwan Singh	1 May 1913	—	—	—

CHAPTER XVII

1914–1921

THE GREAT WAR—FRANCE, 1914-15-16—BACK IN INDIA—
BALUCHISTAN, 1918—THE MARRI RISING—THE DE-
FENCE AT GUMBAZ POST—THE THIRD AFGHAN WAR.

In August 1914 the Regiment was at Meerut peacefully
preparing for the centenary celebrations which were to
be held in the following December, when the Great War
broke out. Meerut was thrown into a state of great excite-
ment, everyone wondering when their particular unit
would receive its orders to mobilise. At last the orders
came for the 7th Meerut Division to mobilise. It was hoped
rather than thought that the order was meant to include
the 7th Meerut Cavalry Brigade, but, to everybody's
bitter disappointment, it was soon made clear that it did
not. Every sign was eagerly examined to see if any
indication of the intention of Army Headquarters could be
found in it. An Indian Army Reserve officer, Lieutenant
Gordon, of the Police, was posted to the Regiment, and
this was promptly interpreted as being a certain sign that
the Regiment was about to receive its orders for France.
Disappointments followed one another in rapid succession,
and four Brigades of Cavalry had left India before at last,
on the 24th October, orders for the Meerut Cavalry
Brigade to mobilise arrived.

The next two days were taken up with medical and
veterinary inspections, and when these were over, the
Regiment was able to report that it could mobilise at full
field service strength, plus a 10 per cent. first reinforcement
without demanding a man or a horse from another unit,
and this after it had already been called upon to supply
various drafts of both men and horses.

On the evening of the 13th November the Regiment entrained at the Meerut City Station for Bombay. The intervening time had been spent drawing mobilisation stores and collecting winter clothing from all over India. On arrival at Bombay on the 16th November, the Brigade went into camp on the Marine Parade, and the next day embarkation began.

Two hired transports, the *Rajah* and the *Ranee*, were allotted to the Regiment; they were the slowest ships in the convoy, but to the men their names appeared as a good omen. Headquarters and "A" and " C " Squadrons embarked on the former, and " B " and " D " Squadrons on the latter. The following officers sailed with the Regiment: Lieutenant-Colonel Wall, Captains Coaker, Vander Gucht, Hulbert, Medlicott, Daniels, Lieutenants Gray, Randall, Gordon, and Broadfoot, and Captain Brierley, the Medical Officer. Captain Polley and Lieutenant Prinsep had been left with the Depôt, which was soon afterwards moved to Bareilly, and Major Gaussen and Lieutenant Lorimer were awaiting the Regiment at Marseilles.

On the 19th November the convoy, consisting of 32 transports, and escorted by the French light cruiser *Dupleix*, sailed. It was still hot, and whilst standing out in the harbour, the horses suffered considerably from the heat. On the 26th November Aden was passed, and on entering the Red Sea with a following breeze, the horses became greatly distressed by the heat. The *Rajah* and *Ranee* were, however, good horseboats, with plenty of room for exercise, and by continued hard work the men, for whom the voyage was a strange experience, kept their horses fit and well. Though there were many cases of fever, the only casualties suffered during the voyage were two horses which died of pneumonia in the Red Sea.

On the 3rd December the convoy reached the Suez, and the next day proceeded up the Canal, which was held by Indian troops. On the 7th December, the centenary of the Regiment, the convoy left Port Said. Throughout the voyage, speculation was rife as to the chances of arriving in France before the War was over. On the 9th the convoy ran into a storm which incapacitated most of the men. On entering the Gulf of Lyons, very heavy weather was encountered and both the *Rajah* and the *Ranee* dropped far behind the rest of the convoy. Marseilles was reached at midday on the 15th December, and disembarkation was begun at once. The Regiment remained for the night in the docks, and the next morning marched through Marseilles to a camp at Saint-Marcel. Here there were only single fly-tents, and as it rained continuously, the men soon received their baptism of European mud and cold. The horses were given gentle exercise to work off the effects of their month at sea.

On the 22nd December the Regiment entrained for Orleans, which had been constituted as sort of an Advanced Base for the Cavalry from India. At every stopping-place throughout the journey demonstrations of welcome and hospitality were met with from the French people, who plied officers and men with hot coffee and cakes. On the evening of the 24th December Orleans was reached, and as soon as detrainment had been completed, the Regiment marched through the city to a camp at La Source, seven miles distant, arriving there early on Christmas morning. There was a hard frost, and settling into camp was comparatively easy ; but the next day a thaw set in, and the camp became a quagmire.

On the arrival of the Meerut and Mhow Cavalry Brigades in France, the Cavalry from India was formed into the Indian Cavalry Corps, under the command of Lieutenant-General " Mike " Rimington. The 1st Indian Cavalry Division, commanded by Major-General Fanshawe, consisted of the Sialkot, Ambala, and Lucknow Brigades ; while the 2nd Indian Cavalry Division, commanded by Major-General Cookson, was formed by the Secunderabad, Meerut, and Mhow Brigades. The Meerut Cavalry, 13th

Hussars, 3rd Skinner's Horse, 18th King George's Own Lancers, and " V " Battery Royal Horse Artillery was commanded by Brigadier-General F. M. Edwards, D.S.O.

A week was spent at Orleans getting the horses into condition and drawing winter clothing. On the 31st December the Brigade received orders to entrain on the following day for an unknown destination. At daybreak on the 2nd January 1915 we woke up to find ourselves travelling along the sea coast, and soon recognised Boulogne. The train moved on slowly through Saint Omer and Aire, and eventually stopped at Burguette, where we were ordered to detrain. Here we were met by our advanced parties, who led us off to Linghem and Liettres, two little country villages about ten miles behind the line. Regimental Headquarters, "A" and " B " Squadrons were billeted in the former, and " C " and " D " Squadrons in the latter. It was our first experience of billeting, and it was not without some difficulty that the men and horses were finally settled in. After a few months, billeting became second nature ; the men soon learnt the ways of our allies and how to make themselves comfortable in this strange country.

One of the first essentials was to get the horses fit and hard. It was, however, evident that " charging time," to use the words of Sir Pertab Singh, was not yet at hand, and the men had to be trained in dismounted action and the methods of trench warfare. During this time it rained and snowed incessantly, and rendered the country difficult to work over. H.R.H. the Prince of Wales on one occasion found "A" and " B " Squadrons out at work and spoke to the Indian officers.

The first piece of work the Brigade was given was to assist in the preparation of a G.H.Q. Line near Robecq, about two miles south-west of Saint-Venant.

The Indian Cavalry Corps had taken over a bit of the line about Festubert, and on the 13th January the Brigade (300 rifles and 2 Vickers guns per Regiment) was moved in buses to Bethune. After a short halt here, the Brigade

10

marched off along the La Bassee Canal to Gorre Bridge, where a halt was made until it was dark. At nightfall the Brigade marched off up the road to Festubert, and here the Regiment received its baptism of fire.

The sector allotted to the Regiment included the village of Le Plantin. The original fire and support trenches had been found untenable, the water in them being waist high, so a line was occupied along the front edge of the village, which the sappers strengthened during the night with breastworks.

During the day the enemy shelled our positions. To prevent the enemy occupying our original fire trenches, the Regiment had been ordered to occupy a small earthwork about 400 yards in front of the line we were holding. The relief of this advanced post had to be carried out under close enemy rifle fire, and with difficulty, as the men at the end of their tour of duty were so cramped and stiff from the cold, that they could only move with assistance. It was during the relief of this post on the morning of the 14th January that the Regiment suffered its first battle casualty in the Great War, Sowar Ali Mohamed, L/B Squadron, being killed. For their conduct on this occasion, Lieutenant E. A. Somerville (22nd Cavalry, attached) and Lance-Dafadar Zahoor Ali were brought to the notice of the Commander-in-Chief, and mentioned in his despatch of the 22nd June 1923.

On the 18th February the whole of the Indian Cavalry Corps was drawn up in line of brigade masses on the downs west of Enquin for inspection by Field-Marshal Sir John French, the Commander-in-Chief of the British Army in France.

During this time the Indian Cavalry Corps was held as a mobile reserve to reinforce any threatened point, and this necessitated units being kept at short notice to move. Four hours was the normal, but at a sign of a threatened attack this was at once reduced to two hours.

At 9 p.m. on the 8th March orders came that the Regi-

ment was to be held at one hour's notice to move. At
2.30 p.m. on the 10th March news was received of our
initial success at Neuve Chapelle, and at 11.30 p.m. orders
came that the Brigade would rendezvous at Estrée Blanche
at 4.30 a.m. the next morning. By daylight the 11th
March the Indian Cavalry Corps was concentrated in the
woods about Lapugnoy. Concealed from hostile aircraft,
the Corps lay in these woods for three days, ready to gallop
for the gap as soon as our Infantry had breached the
German line. At 1.30 p.m. on the 12th information was
received that the German counter-attack on our newly
gained position had been beaten off, but the following day
all hope of a break-through was abandoned, and at nightfall the Corps moved back. About midnight 13th/14th
March the Regiment reached its billets, the Headquarters
being at Lambres on the main road between Bethune and
Aire.

On the 18th March the Brigade moved back west of
Aire, Regimental Headquarters being billeted at Rac-
quinham. Fine spring weather had favoured us during
the operations, but on the 19th March there was a heavy
fall of snow and it became bitterly cold. Working parties
were again employed on the construction of G.H.Q. Reserve
Line near Robecq. On the 15th April three Yeomanry
officers, Captains O'Hara and Heath and Lieutenant
Little, joined the Regiment for duty.

At 10 a.m. on the 23rd April, whilst the Brigade was
engaged in a tactical exercise, news was brought to the
Brigadier of the Gas Attack at Ypres, and that the British
Cavalry Corps had already received its orders to be in
readiness to move. The Brigade returned at once to billets
to await orders. Nothing more happened this day ; but
at 4.15 p.m. on the 24th, orders suddenly arrived to march
at once, and Squadrons had to gallop to the Brigade start-
ing-point, Wardecques Station, to be there in time. Under
cover of darkness the Indian Cavalry Corps moved towards Ypres. That night it halted near Cassel, the Regi-

ment bivouacking in a meadow at Le Tom, which was reached about 9.30 p.m.   The Corps lay round Cassel the three following days at an hour's notice to move.   At 12.15 p.m. on the 28th April, orders arrived to move at once.   The 2nd Division moved via Wemaers–Cappel–Hardifort, and Hout–Kerque, where the Belgian frontier was crossed.   Thence the march was continued to the westwards of Ypres, the Regiment going into bivouac at Proven on the Poperinghe Road.   The 29th April was a beautiful warm spring day and was a welcome change to the bitter cold that had been experienced in bivouac round Cassel.

On the 1st May three officers' patrols from the Regiment under Captain Daniels carried out part of a divisional reconnaissance of the roads and country from our bivouac area to the advanced allied line :   right patrol, Captain Heath ; centre patrol, Captain Molloy ; left patrol, Second Lieutenant Broadfoot.   The area allotted to the Brigade lay between the Ypres–Furnes Road and the Yser Canal. The Regiment was given the right section, right boundary railway bridge over canal to near Brielen, left boundary Elverdinghe–Het Sas on the canal.   Patrols left Proven at 6 a.m. and marched via Poperinghe to Elverdinghe, which was reached at 7.30 a.m.   Here these patrols were despatched to their various tasks.   Patrols penetrated up to French front lines which ran along the south bank of the canal ; the last part of the advance had to be carried out dismounted, being under close observation from the German lines.   The enemy's artillery shelled the area briskly during the reconnaissance.   Broadfoot's patrol had been directed on Het Sas, but on reaching the French advanced line found the enemy in possession of both banks of the canal at this point.

On the morning of the 2nd May the Corps commenced its return march to Cassel, the Regiment bivouacking that night again at Le Tom.   On the morning of the 4th May the Corps moved back under cover of darkness to the vicinity of Aire, the Regiment going into billets at Rely, but, owing to the scarcity of water at this village, was moved on the 6th May to Enquin and Cerney.

On the 8th May orders were received to be ready to move at 5 a.m. the next morning. No orders were received that day, but the horses were kept saddled up and transport ready to move at a moment's notice. The big French attack on the Vimy Ridge had been launched and the British Army was making a holding attack at Festubert. On the 14th May notice to move was increased to four hours. At 10 a.m. on the 16th notice to move was reduced to two hours, and at 2 p.m. on the 17th orders were received " to move at once." The Corps marched as rapidly as possible to the woods at Lapugnoy, where it had waited in March during the Battle of Neuve-Chapelle for the break-through. It rained incessantly, and as all baggage had been dumped at billets to free " B " Echelon Transport for the carriage of reserve rations, the men were without their waterproof sheets.

The Corps waited in these woods until the 19th May, when, again to everyone's great disappointment, the hope of a break-through had to be given up and orders were issued for the return to billets.

On the 23rd May Captain R. W. Manderson joined the Regiment with a draft from H.E. the Governor-General of India's Bodyguard. For the next month the weather was warm and fine and the horses improved in condition on the ample grazing that was available along the wayside of the country lanes and roads.

On the 28th June a working party of 230 men under Major Gaussen was despatched in buses to Nœux-les-Mines for work on the trench system behind Vermelles, opposite Loos. Work here was no sinecure. From the Eifel Tower at Loos, the working parties were in full view of the Boche gunners, who did not fail to " strafe " them both at work and in their billets. This party returned on the 2nd July.

On the 8th July the Indian Cavalry Corps was drawn up on the Linghem Downs for inspection by Lord Kitchener. The Field-Marshal, who was accompanied by Sir Douglas Haig, rode round the whole Corps and addressed a few words to each unit, speaking in Urdu to the Indian officers.

On the 10th July a second working party was sent up to Nœux-les-Mines, this time being billeted at Les Brebis. Owing to enemy shell fire it was found necessary to set the men to work before daylight, so that they could get underground before the morning " strafe " began and continue work under cover.

On the 18th July 200 men returned to billets, and from the 20th onwards Regiments were ordered to maintain a permanent working party of 160 men, to be relieved weekly.

On the 27th July the Indian Cavalry Corps was ordered to join the newly-formed Third Army, which was taking over a portion of the French Line between Arras and the Somme.

On the 1st August the Corps marched southwards, the Regiment bivouacking at Maresque in a meadow on the banks of the River Canche. The inhabitants were most friendly and the Maire gave a large dinner party in honour of Regimental Headquarters, which were billeted in his house. The next day the route lay past the famous battlefield of Crecy, Domvast, and Saint-Riquier to Ailly–le Haut–Clocher, where the Regiment went into bivouac. It was a hot, trying march of over thirty miles and water for the horses was scarce. The next day the march was continued in pouring rain, via Mouflers and Flexicourt to Hangest-sur-Somme, where the Brigade Headquarters and the Regiment went into billets.

The Indian Cavalry Corps had taken over a sector of the line opposite Thiepval, and on the 8th August orders were received for the Brigade, 300 rifles and 2 Vickers guns per Regiment to go up the following day in buses to Baizieux.

At 8 p.m. on the 9th August the Brigade " embused " and moved under cover of darkness to Hedauville.

Baizieux was six miles farther on, but as it was getting light the buses refused to go any further and the remainder of the journey had to be completed on foot.

The Brigade remained in close billets at Baizieux throughout the 10th and 11th of August. At 9 p.m. on the 12th August it marched under cover of darkness to Martinsart, where it remained throughout the next day. Here the Brigade was formed into a Battalion of six companies, each Regiment forming two companies of four platoons or half squadrons. Brigade Headquarters returned to billets, and the command of this Battalion devolved on Colonel Grimston, 18th King George's Own Lancers, the senior commanding officer. Regimental Headquarters remained, the company formed from the right wing was commanded by Captain Raban and that from the left wing by Captain Coaker. The Secunderabad, Mhow, and Sialkot Brigades, which had either come up or were being brought up, were likewise formed into provisional Battalions. The four Battalions thus formed were placed under the orders of Brigadier-General Wadeson, Commanding the Secunderabad Cavalry Brigade, and were detailed to take over the trenches held by the 152nd Brigade, 51st Highland Division (T.).

Company Commanders spent the night 12th/13th August in the trenches they were to take over, and Colonel Wall went up early the next morning. At 8 p.m. the relief commenced and was completed by 12.30 a.m.

The Regiment remained in the line until the 24th August. The enemy kept up the desultory fire of a quiet sector and our casualties amounted to 5 I.O.R.s wounded only. The men were kept hard at work the whole time repairing and improving the trenches, and at night patrols reconnoitred the enemy's wire.

One point occupied our special attention. We could hear the enemy hard at work, constructing something in their front line, and every night patrols were sent out to try to ascertain what it was.   Later it transpired that it was the commencement of the famous " Leipzig Redoubt."   A curious incident which occurred whilst we were in the line was the putting up by the enemy of "blue and yellow " lance pennons, exactly opposite our position.

On the 21st August Captain Daniels was appointed Staff-Captain, the Mhow Cavalry Brigade, vice Captain Wylly, V.C., of the Guides, wounded, and handed over the Adjutancy of the Regiment to Lieutenant Gray.

On the night 24th/25th August, the Regiment was relieved by the 9th Hodson's Horse, and marched back via Martinsart to Forceville, where the horses which had been brought up from billets were waiting.   The march was then continued to Montigny, which was reached at 5.30 a.m. and here the Brigade went into billets.   The next day the horses were sent back to Hangest, the men being employed in the preparation of a reserve line about Senlis, just behind Albert.

On the 1st September the horses were brought up again and the provisional Battalion from the Brigade, this time commanded by Colonel Wall, returned for another tour of duty in the trenches.   The Regiment on this occasion relieved the 19th Lancers in the left sub-sector of the Brigade front.   The line occupied by the Regiment was directly opposite Thiepval Château.   It ran for some distance along the circular drive around the château, and the right formed a small salient which extended to within forty yards of the enemy's trenches.   There had been heavy rain, and the trenches were deep in mud.   On the night 3rd/4th September the enemy opened with trench mortars and blew in a portion of the front line held by " B " Squadron.   The German guns and trench mortars were distinctly active throughout this tour of duty in the trenches.   On the 6th September, Risaldar Mukand Singh was wounded by shell fire.

Enemy snipers from the trees round the château

harassed our lines, but these were dispersed by machine-gun fire. On the night 7th/8th the enemy again blew in the trenches in the salient with trench mortars, Risaldar Nur Muhammed and four I.O.R.s being wounded. The next day two more I.O.R.s were wounded. On the night 10th/11th September, Lieutenant Randall and Lance-Dafadar Kehar Singh crawled out into the wood and located two machine-gun posts which had been giving trouble. Our Artillery knocked these out the following day. On the 11th September the enemy brought a heavier mortar into action, and did considerable damage to the parapet. On the night 12th/13th September the Regiment was relieved by the 19th Lancers. Squadrons marched back independently to Englebelmar, where the horses had been brought, and the Regiment then returned to Montigny. One hundred diggers with their horses were left at Montigny, and after dark on the 13th September the Regiment returned to Hangest. On the 14th September the Brigade billeting area was changed, the Regiment moving to Alléry. On the 21st Lord Kitchener inspected the Indian Cavalry Corps. Gossip from Divisional Headquarters led us to believe that divisional training was to take place. In reality the Battle of Loos was about to open, and three Cavalry Corps—Conneau's, the British, and the Indian—were to be concentrated round Saint-Pol. Here they were to be held in readiness to exploit any success that might be achieved.

On the 22nd the Corps moved northwards, the Regiment going into close billets at Berneuil. Here special arrangements were organised for the maintenance of supplies in the event of the Corps getting through the German lines. On the 25th September orders were received to be ready to move at one and a half hour's notice. News of the progress of the great battle leaked through, but, to everyone's great disappointment, the order to advance never came. On the 1st October the Regiment moved to Berneuil. Risaldar Balwant Singh was appointed Risaldar

Major vice Risaldar Major Ashraf Ali Khan, Bahadur, who returned to India.

On the 14th October the Regiment commenced its return march to the last billeting area. It remained about eight days at Houzecourt, and on the 22nd October was back in Alléry.

During the winter 1915–16 nothing worthy of record occurred. Each Cavalry Division had one mounted Brigade in readiness for action, the remaining two Brigades being organised into provisional Infantry Battalions. Working parties were employed preparing new trench systems on the 3rd Army Front, and the winter passed without incident. On the 5th November Major Gaussen left to take command of a service Battalion.

On the 17th November the Regiment was moved from Alléry to an area Tours-en-Vimeu, Hamicourt, Longue-mort, and Carroy (Somme). On the 3rd February billets were again changed, Headquarters moving to Courcelles, "A" and "C" Squadrons to Aigneville, "B" to Courtieux, "D" remaining at Carroy.

On the 13th March an unfortunate accident occurred whilst "B" Squadron were doing bomb practice. It resulted in the death of Captain Heath and Lance-Dafadar Imam Ali Khan, while Jemadar Ashraf Khan and several men were wounded.

On the 11th April the Brigade moved to Saint-Riquier for ten days' brigade training. The machine-gun sections had now been withdrawn from Regiments and formed into Brigade machine-gun squadrons, Hotchkiss guns being issued to squadrons.

Our working parties lately had been employed under the orders of the 13th Corps in preparation for the Battle of the Somme, and while there, on the 7th June, Sowar Maru Singh was killed. On the 26th May the Regiment had moved to Beauchamps in the Valley of the Bresle, within ten miles of the sea.

On the 27th May, Brigadier-General L. C. Jones, C.M.G.,

M.V.O., succeeded Brigadier-General F. M. Edwards, D.S.O., on the latter being transferred to the command of the 71st Infantry Brigade. On the 2nd June the first issue of steel helmets was made to the Regiment.

On the 10th June the Brigade was back at Saint-Riquier for ten days' training. On the 14th June, just as the Brigade was starting out on a tactical exercise, a message was received to return to billets at once, and it transpired later that the Brigade was to go to Mesopotamia. As the 18th Lancers were composed chiefly of Mohammedans, they were replaced in the Meerut Brigade by the 30th Lancers.

On the 20th June the Regiment entrained at Pont Remy for Marseilles. As it passed through Amiens, the preliminary bombardment of the Battle of the Somme commenced. On the 24th June the left wing, under Major Coaker, embarked on h.t. *Missourie*, followed on the 7th July by the remainder of the Regiment on h.t. *Kingstonian*.

A voyage through the Red Sea, with horses, in iron ships, at this time of the year, was no mean undertaking, and doubts were freely expressed at the start as to whether 25 per cent. of the horses would reach Bombay alive. However, by dint of hard work and care, the Regiment only lost thirty horses.

On arrival at Bombay it was discovered that both the Indian Regiments in the Brigade were to remain in India, being replaced by the 13th and 14th Lancers, who had not as yet had an opportunity of seeing foreign service. The Regiment was ordered to Rawal Pindi, where it was finally concentrated on the 6th August 1916.

Captain Daniels and Captain Metcalfe accompanied the 7th Meerut Cavalry Brigade Headquarters to Mesopotamia, and a large number of men of the Regiment volunteered to stay on with the Brigade Signal Troop and Machine-gun Squadron. Among the latter was Jemadar Amin Lall, Bahadur, who won the Military Cross. Other

British officers and Indian ranks soon followed as drafts to various units in Mesopotamia, where they well maintained the good name of the Regiment.   Dafadar (later Risaldar) Jowahir Singh, who was attached to the 32nd Lancers, gained the Indian Order of Merit, 2nd Class, for conspicuous gallantry, as did also Jemadar Indar Singh, attached to the 7th Meerut Divisional Signal Company. Lieutenant Prinsep returned to France, where he was attached to the 18th Lancers.   He was wounded shortly after arrival in an action on the Somme, and had to be sent back to India.

In Mesopotamia, Major Hulbert joined the 10th Hodson's Horse, Captain Manderson the 12th Cavalry, Captain Lorimer the Remount Depot, and Major Stokes, who started as G.S.O. (1) Intelligence, Baghdad, finished up the war as British High Commissioner of the Caucasus.

Major Webber, who had taken the Jaipur Transport Corps to Mesopotamia in 1914, joined the 16th Cavalry when that Regiment was short of British officers, and was severely wounded at the Battle of Shaiba on the 14th April 1915.   Major Medlicott remained in France until the end of the war on the staff of the Cavalry Corps. Major Conway-Gordon, who went out to France in 1914 as G.S.O. (2), 1st Indian Cavalry Division, was transferred in 1916 to the 12th Infantry Division, but with many other Indian Army officers was recalled to India in 1917.

For his services in command of the Regiment in France, Lieutenant-Colonel Wall was awarded the C.M.G., being subsequently promoted full Colonel.   Risaldar Major Balwant Singh received the Order of British India, 2nd Class, for distinguished service in the field, and was promoted three years later to the 1st Class.

In August 1917 the Regiment was moved from Rawal Pindi to Jullundur.   It only remained here a few months, being ordered in October to Loralai.

Early in 1918 trouble began to brew in the Marri country.   On the 17th February it was decided to reinforce the detachment that the Regiment furnished at Gumbaz Post, and Major Gaussen, who had recently rejoined the Regiment from France, was ordered to proceed there with 50 men. On arrival at Gumbaz on the 18th February, Gaussen found all quiet and the Political Officer living in the bungalow some distance from the Fort ; but towards evening he decided that all was not well, and persuaded the Political Officer to move into the Fort. Up to this time the Marris had committed no open act of hostility, but at 11 p.m. on 19th February, without any warning, the Fort was attacked with a violence almost unprecedented in the history of frontier warfare. With the small number of men at his disposal, Gaussen had decided that it was impossible to hold the whole perimeter and had concentrated his men for the defence of the two flanking towers. The total number he had at his disposal only amounted to 80 men of "A," " C," and " D " Squadrons, and while he himself took command of one tower, he detached Lieutenant H. H. Lyons to the command of the other.

Urged on by their mullahs, who had promised them immunity from the " bullets of the infidels," the Marris came on in their hundreds, armed with swords only. They scaled the perimeter walls and hurled themselves against the towers. The first attack was beaten off, only to be renewed with redoubled vigour a few minutes later. This attack, like the first, was repulsed with heavy loss, but at 2 a.m. the Marris made a third and final attempt to take the Fort. Again they failed, and this was enough for the Marris, and they withdrew showering curses on the infidels. It is not known how many of their wounded they carried away, but 200 dead and wounded were counted lying in and around the Fort the next morning. This action broke the back of the Marri Rising. A column visited their country later, but not a shot was fired.

Large as this little incident may loom in the history of the 3rd Skinner's Horse, few outside the Regiment have heard of it, but it is gratifying to know that the " Defence of Gumbaż Post " has been considered worthy of inclusion in the Official List of Battles and Actions of the Great War.

For their services in this affair, Major Gaussen received the C.I.E., Lieutenant Lyons the M.C., and Dafadar Lall Singh (killed) and Lance-Dafadar Khem Singh, the Indian Order of Merit, 2nd Class.

In 1918 six extra Indian Cavalry Regiments were raised, squadrons of the Regiment providing their quotas as follows: A, 1 squadron; B, ½ squadron; D, ½ squadron; these were drafted to the new 40th Cavalry, the command of which was given to Major Gaussen.

Later in the same year Colonel E. W. Wall, C.M.G., vacated the command of the Regiment on his appointment as Base Commandant, Bushire. Major J. R. Gaussen, C.M.G., C.I.E., D.S.O., was appointed Commandant, but remained in command of the 40th Cavalry, the command of the Regiment devolving on Major Coaker.

The Regiment was still at Loralai in May 1919 when the Third Afghan War broke out. On the 24th May " C " and " D " Squadrons, under Major Vander Gucht, were ordered to march to Kila Saifulla in the Zhob. There had been no tribal rising up to that time, but it was thought that the presence of troops would have a salutary effect.

An incident which happened immediately on the arrival of the Squadrons at Kila Saifulla is worthy of note, not only on account of the gallantry and initiative shown by those who participated in it, but also because it resulted in the complete overawal of the tribes in the neighbourhood of that place.

There lived in the vicinity a somewhat notorious firebrand, by name Baz Khan, whom the Extra Assistant Commissioner at Kila Saifulla had been ordered to arrest. Baz Khan had on several occasions been summoned to

Kila Saifulla for this purpose, but on each occasion his arrest had proved too terrifying a proposition, it being fully realised that he would certainly put up a fight before his capture. On the day of the arrival of " C " and " D " Squadrons the Extra Assistant Commissioner had sent for him, but had again failed to make him prisoner. As the transport arrived at the courtyard of the Fort, it happened that Baz Khan was making his departure. Alarmed possibly at the sudden arrival of troops, or perhaps fearing a trap, he leapt on a pony which was standing in the bazaar and made a dash for safety. His hurried departure caused considerable commotion, which was of course heard by the Squadrons, which were a short distance away watering their horses, and by the escort to the transport, who had not yet unsaddled. Among the former was Lance-Dafadar Pritam Singh and among the latter Lance-Dafadar Gurdyal Singh and Sowar Chajja Singh. On ascertaining what the hubbub was about they all, without any orders, mounted and set off in pursuit, Pritam Singh riding bareback, having hastily snatched a lance.

After galloping about three miles over very broken country, the three came up with Baz Khan, whose horse was exhausted and could go no farther. They found him waiting for them in a nullah with a Colt automatic in his hand. Chajja Singh at once charged with a lance, but missed and got a shot in the shoulder. Pritam Singh next went for him, but also missed. His horse was shot, and he received a graze across the stomach. Gurdyal Singh, with a sword, managed to sever Baz Khan's right wrist, but also had his horse shot in the neck. Gurdyal Singh then dismounted and managed to get hold of Baz Khan. The two were locked in a death struggle when Jemadar Mangal Singh and some half-dozen more men arrived and shot Baz Khan.

For their conduct on this occasion Gurdyal Singh and Pritam Singh were awarded the I.D.S.M., and all three men received a sum of money from the Political Agent. Chajja Singh unfortunately contracted fever as a result of his wound, and had to be evacuated to Karachi, where he died in hospital.

On the 5th June "A" and " B " Squadrons were ordered to Murgha. On the 9th June Lieutenant Macqueen with one troop "A" Squadron escorted Major Bruce—the Political Agent at Loralai—to Musa Khel, where they arrived that night. Early the following morning they were attacked by tribesmen. The enemy's attack was beaten off with loss, estimated at about 10 killed and wounded, the Hotchkiss gun being used with good effect. At 2 p.m. a plane flew over Musa Khel, causing the tribesmen to disperse, and no further fighting took place. In his report of the action, Major Bruce highly commended the conduct of Lieutenant Macqueen and the troop under his command.

On the 12th June Lieutenant Fraser with a troop from " D " Squadron escorted Captain Finnis, the Assistant Political Officer, to Gwal Haiderazai. From here a report was sent back to the Regiment that Gwal Haiderazai was about to be attacked, and Lieutenant Anderson was despatched at once with the remainder of " D " Squadron to their assistance. After an all-night march Anderson reached the Fort, only to find that the report of an impending attack had been proved to be groundless.

All this time preparations were being made for the advance of the striking force from Chaman on Kandahar. In July the Regiment was ordered to Chaman, and on the 22nd "A" and " B " Squadrons marched to Harnai, where they entrained on the 25th. " C " and " D " Squadrons were still at Kila Saifulla when the orders came. " D " was ordered to rejoin the Regimental Headquarters at Harnai, whilst " C " was ordered to Hindu Bagh. On arrival at Yaru Karez " B " Squadron was ordered to detrain and remain at Pishin. Regimental Headquarters and "A" Squadron proceeding to Chaman, which was reached on the 26th July.

The armistice was signed on the 9th September 1919, and the Regiment returned to Quetta in October. For his services during this critical period on the Frontier, Major V. A. Coaker was awarded the D.S.O.

Shortly after the return to Quetta the Regiment was warned for service in Palestine. All the men were sent away on three months' leave, but shortly afterwards the order was cancelled, and the Regiment moved down to Sibi for the winter. In the spring of 1920 the Regiment returned to Quetta. In April, owing to another Afghan scare, the Regiment, under Major S. T. Polley, was hurried up to Chaman, but returned to Quetta again in July.

In October 1920 the Regiment moved in relief to Sialkot. Lieutenant-Colonel (temporary Brigadier-General) Gaussen, who for the last twelve months had been commanding the Brigade at Meshed, retired this year, and was succeeded in command of the Regiment by Lieutenant-Colonel E. C. W. Conway-Gordon, C.I.E. This officer had recently returned from Warizistan, where he had been serving as G.S.O. (1), Derajat Column.

Instructions for the conversion of silladar regiments to the present organisation soon followed, and in 1921 the two Regiments of Skinner's Horse were amalgamated.

Risaldar Major and Honorary Lieutenant Sheochand, Sirdar Bahadur, retired and was succeeded by Risaldar Nur Mohammad, Bahadur.

No history of the 3rd Skinner's Horse would be complete without some reference to two striking personalities who have for so many years been connected with the Regiment. There cannot be an officer living who can remember the day when there was not a Gopal Das in the Adjutant's office, or a Jai Kishen, the accountant, to whom to turn for information. Reared in the old school, these two

11

clerks have handed down to many generations the high traditions they inherited. Officers have come and gone, but all through the upheaval caused by the Great War these two old gentlemen stuck to their posts. The day, perhaps, has yet to come when it will be fully realised how much they have done for the Regiment.

Extract from Indian Army List "January 1923"

1ST DUKE OF YORK'S OWN SKINNER'S HORSE

[Late 1st D.Y.O. Lancers (Skinner's Horse) and 3rd Skinner's Horse, amalgamated 1921.]

Present designation, 1922.

Composition.—1 Squadron of Hindustani Musalmans and Musalman Rajputs, 1 of Rajputs of Eastern Punjab and United Provinces, 1 of Jats.

Ferozepore.

Colonel-in-Chief—THE KING.

Colonel—Major-General P. HOLLAND-PRYOR, C.B., C.M.G., D.S.O., M.V.O.

Honorary Colonel—Hon. Lieutenant-General *His Highness Sir Madho Rao Scindia, Bahadur, G.C.S.I., G.C.V.O., G.B.E., A.-D.-C., Maharaja of Gwalior,* 1 Jan. 1906.

First Commission.	Names and Rank.	Army Rank.	Remarks.
	COMMANDANT.		
16 Jan. 1895	Lieutenant-Colonel E. C. W. Conway-Gordon, C.I.E., p.s.c.	29 May 1920	—
	SQUADRON COMMANDERS AND OFFICERS.		
4 Aug. 1897	Major M. R. H. Webber	4 Aug. 1915	D.A.D.R.T., *Wazir force.*
22 Jan. 1898	Major V. A. Coaker, D.S.O.	1 Sept. 1915	Second in Command.
18 July 1900	Brevet Lieutenant-Colonel J. A. Muirhead, D.S.O., *p.s.c.*	3 June 1919	*Lt. ex I.*
8 Jan. 1901	*Major E. H. Pott,* D.S.O.	8 Jan. 1916	Military Adviser, I.S. Forces, Jaipur.
22 Oct. 1902	Major S. T. Polley	22 Oct. 1917	—
22 July 1903	Major H. Gillies	12 Dec. 1917	—
22 July 1903	Major G. A. C. Wetherall	22 July 1918	—
18 Jan. 1905	Major A. M. Daniels, O.B.E., *p.s.c.*	10 Mar. 1917	—
24 Jan. 1905	Major A. A. H. Beaman, D.S.O.	25 Aug. 1920	*Lt. ex I., m.c., to 5 June 23.*
5 Aug. 1906	Major J. M. Lorimer	24 Jan. 1921	*Lt. ex I., m.c., to 5 June 23.*
17 Aug. 1907	*Major E. D. Metcalfe, M.V.O., M.C.*	17 *Aug.* 1922	*Ty. Equerry to H.R.H. the Prince of Wales.*
9 Sept. 1908	Captain G. C. G. Gray (s.c.)	1 Sept. 1915	Qr. Mr. (Offg.)
2 Sept. 1910	Captain M. M. Stevenson	1 Sept. 1915	Adjt. and Qr. Mr. I. A. Sch. of Edn.
25 Sept. 1911	Captain B. Fitz H. Randall	25 Sept. 1915	*Lt. ex I., to 15 June 23.*
24 Aug. 1912	Captain A. D. Magnay (s.c.)	24 Aug. 1916	—
25 *Aug.* 1917	Captain Zorawar Singh, M.C.	25 Aug. 1917	With I.S. Forces.
14 Jan. 1914	Captain Aga Cassim Shah	14 Jan. 1917	With 2-9 Jat. R.
18 Jan. 1914	Captain W. A. Broadfoot	14 Jan. 1918	—
8 Aug. 1914	*Captain E. V. Fulton*	8 Aug. 1918	G.S.O., 3rd gr. (Intell.) N. Comd.
5 *May* 1915	Captain D. W. M. Prinsep	*Jan.* 1918	—
6 May 1915	*Captain A. R. Jefferis*	3 *May* 1919	*Staff Captain, Wazir force.*
Sept. 1915	Captain E. L. Turner	5 May 1919	Adjutant (Offg.)
15 Nov. 1915	Captain A. E. Turner	6 *Sept.* 1919	*Asst. Adjt.-Gen., N. Comd. (Offg.)*
15 Nov. 1915	Captain A. D. Wilson	15 Nov. 1919	*Asst. Minister of Defence, Iraq. Govt.*
18 Nov. 1915	*Captain J. M. Stapylton*	15 Nov. 1919	With Assam Rif.
18 Apl. 1916	Captain J. L. Muir	18 Nov. 1919	A.D.C. to Govr. of U.P.
21 May 1916	Captain H. G. Bell	18 Apl. 1920	With Ind. Sig. Corps.
27 Apl. 1917	Captain B. L. C. L. Mills, M.C.	21 *May* 1920	R.E. Iraq.
	Lieutenant V. C. A. Munckton	27 Jan. 1919	With N. Comd. Hdqrs.

Lieutenant R. F. Gruar .	1 June 1917	1 Mar. 1919	With Ind. Sig. Corps.
Lieutenant R. B. Macqueen .	24 Apl. 1918	24 Apl. 1919	Attd.
Lieutenant K. C. Cradock-Watson .	24 Aug. 1918	21 Aug. 1919	With Ind. Sig. Corps.
Lieutenant R. Wilson .	6 Apl. 1918	6 Jan. 1920	Cav. Sch., Saugor. —
Lieutenant R. H. G. Prettejohn .	16 July 1920	16 July 1921	—

HONORARY OFFICER.

Hon. Major S. E. Skinner .	10 Feb. 1893	10 Feb. 1920	Not attached for duty.

INDIAN OFFICERS

Date of entering Service.	Names.	Dates of Commission as Jemadar.	Ressaidar.	Risaldar.	Remarks.
	RISALDAR MAJOR.				
16 Jan. 1894	Nur Muhammad Khan, Bahadur (56, 66a, 71)	1 Jan. 1905	16 Oct. 1910	22 Sept. 1915	Risaldar Major 1 Aug. 1920. Order of Br. I., 2nd Class.
	RISALDARS.				
3 Jan. 1901	Ral Singh (45a, 56, 71)	15 Feb. 1911	24 Oct. 1914	6 Oct. 1915	—
1 May 1892	Faujdar Khan, Bahadur (66a)	10 Nov. 1906	8 Dec. 1915	21 Nov. 1917	Order of Br. I., 2nd Class.
1 May 1892	Barkat Khan (56, 66a)	1 Oct. 1908	5 July 1915	1 Nov. 1920	—
1 Feb. 1886		16 Aug. 1911	1 Jan. 1918	1 Apl. 1921	—
13 Apl. 1889	Habibur Rahman Khan (Hon. Lieutenant) C.I.E., Khan Sahib, Bahadur.	5 Nov. 1912	4 Apl. 1917		Order of Br. I., 2nd Class. Asst. Translation Offr. and Asst. Editor, "Fauji Akhbar," A. Hdqrs.
	JEMADARS.				
10 Feb. 1903	Amar Singh	3 Jan. 1918	1 Feb. 1920	1 Apl. 1921	
1 Feb. 1909	Amin Lall, M.C. (45a, 61)	28 Dec. 1916	1 Aug. 1920	1 Apl. 1912	
18 Dec. 1903	Badshah Husain (56)	3 Apl. 1917	1 Aug. 1920	1 Apl. 1921	With Sistan Levee.
1 Dec. 1903	Bhagwan Singh (47a, 56, 126a)	1 Jan. 1918	1 Aug. 1920	1 Apl. 1921	
3 July 1899	Asghar Ali Khan	3 Jan. 1918	1 Aug. 1920	1 Apl. 1921	
19 Apl. 1900	Wali Muhammad Khan	22 May 1917	1 Aug. 1920	1 May 1921	
1 Jan. 1897	Murtaza Khan (56)	5 Apl. 1915	—	—	Indian Qr.-Mr.
1 Nov. 1894	Sher Muhammad Khan (56)	5 July 1915	—	—	
16 Apl. 1901	Ratan Singh (56, 66a)	10 Nov. 1916	—	—	Adjt. and Qr.-Mr., Rest Camp, Khirgi.
16 Jan. 1906	Farzand Ali Khan (45a, 56)	8 Jan. 1918	—	—	
1 Apl. 1903	Mohan Singh	20 Feb. 1918	—	—	
16 May 1913	Ghulam Rasul Khan (50a)	10 May 1919	—	—	
17 May 1913	Raghbir Singh (47, 52, 56)	1 May 1920	—	—	
1 Mar. 1912	Nur Muhammad Khan (45a, 52, 56)	1 Feb. 1920	—	—	Woordie Major.
2 Oct. 1902	Kehar Singh	1 May 1921	—	—	
1 Jan. 1891	Jai Krishan Singh (126)		—	—	Chief Clerk.
	ATTACHED.				
1 July 1917	Kamyab Khan, Jemadar (126a) .	18 Apl. 1922	—	—	I.A.E.C.

APPENDIX A

THE EVOLUTION OF A REGIMENT OF INDIAN CAVALRY (BENGAL ARMY)

In 1760 Clive felt the necessity for Cavalry in his expeditions against the Shahzada, and consequently Major Caillaud, whom he had placed in command of the Army, caused two troops of European Dragoons and one of Hussars to be raised from the European Infantry. He also succeeded in raising two Risalahs of Cavalry, called the Mohgal Horse, composed of, and officered entirely by Indians, who provided their own horses, arms, and accoutrements, and received Rs.50 a month pay.

The latter could not have attained a very high standard of efficiency, as, in his report of about 1770, the Commander-in-Chief said : "The black Cavalry are at present of no further use than to attend the Commander-in-Chief and Colonels of Brigades, and are too inconsiderable to be of service in time of war ; for I know by experience it is impossible from the viciousness of the horses to discipline Cavalry here to any tolerable degree of perfection, and castrating the horses ruins their spirit."

A G.O.C.C. dated the 2nd June 1796 introduced a complete reorganisation of the Bengal Army. In this was included the provision for four Regiments of Regular Native Cavalry of six troops each. Each Regiment when completed was commanded by a Field Officer and consisted of :

2 Captains	STAFF.
1 Captain-Lieutenant	1 Adjutant
6 Lieutenants	1 Quartermaster
3 Cornets	1 Paymaster
2 Sergeants	1 Surgeon's mate
6 Subadars	1 Sergeant-Major
6 Jemadars	1 Quartermaster-Sergeant
18 Havildars	1 Drill Havildar
18 Naiks	1 Drill Naik
6 Trumpeters	1 Trumpet Major
420 Troopers	1 Native Doctor

APPENDIX A 167

In 1800 two additional Regiments of Regular Native
Cavalry were raised, namely, the 5th and 6th Light Cavalry,
and in the same year orders were issued that two six-pounder
field pieces called "Galloper guns" were to be attached to
each regiment of Cavalry.

Later, in 1803, a letter was received from the Court of Direc-
tors, dated 20th April 1803, in which was expressed a deter-
mination to assimilate the organisation of the Regular Native
Cavalry as much as possible to that of the Infantry. For
this purpose orders were issued that two Regiments should
constitute a Brigade commanded by a Colonel; at the same
time a considerable addition was made to the strength of the
regular Regiments, which were now composed as follows :

1 Lieutenant-Colonel	6 Trumpeters
1 Major	492 Privates
2 Captains	6 Farriers
1 Captain-Lieutenant	6 Pakhalis
6 Lieutenants	1 Surgeon
6 Cornets	1 Riding Master
6 Subadars	1 Quartermaster-Sergeant
12 Jemadars	1 Assistant Surgeon
24 Havildars	1 Native Doctor
24 Naiks	1 Sergeant-Major

In the same year, 1803, the Mahratta War broke out, and the
story has been told in Part I of how on the fall of Delhi a
body of Scindia's Cavalry came over to the British and was
given service under Captain James Skinner, as Captain Skinner's
Irregular Horse.

The campaigns against the Mahrattas and Pindaris with
their vast hordes of horsemen showed the Honourable East
India Company the necessity of increasing its Cavalry, and
further Corps of Irregular Horse similar to Skinner's Horse
were raised, chiefly by half-pay officers.

In February 1809 (G.O.C.C., 1st February), orders were issued
for the rendezvous at Sonpat and Panipat of all the irregular
horse in the employ of Government ; the whole to be commanded by Major James Skinner. At the same time a further
enlistment for that officer's Regiment was ordered. Three
months later (Proclamation G.C., 29th May 1809) Skinner's
Horse was augmented to a strength of eight Risalahs with

Galloper guns attached. The strength and rates of pay of a Risalah are given below :

		Rs.
Risaldar .	. . . .	80
Naib Risaldar .	. . . .	50
Jemadar	. . . .	45
Kot Dafadar .	. . . .	35
5 Dafadars @ .	. . . .	28
Nishan Bardar.	. . . .	28
Nagarchi.	. . . .	25
100 Sowars @ .	. . . .	20
Vakil .	. . . .	20
2 Bhistis @	. . . .	5

In 1815 (G.O.C.C., 29th July) the establishment of Skinner's Horse was augmented to three Corps of 1,000 Sowars each, with the following Staff and Officers :

1 Captain
5 Lieutenants
5 Cornets
10 Risaldars
10 Naib Risaldars
10 Jemadars
10 Kot Dafadars
80 Dafadars
10 Nishanchis
10 Nagarchis
10 Vakils
100 Bhistis

1 Havildar ⎫
1 Naik ⎬ To work the Galloper Guns.
41 Sepoys ⎭

The three Corps of Rohilla Cavalry, commanded by Lieutenant Roberts, Captain Cunningham, and Captain Baddeley, were also placed on the above establishment, with the exception of the Galloper guns. In 1809 (G.O.C.C., 12th May) another Corps of Irregular Cavalry had been raised for provincial work in the ceded and conquered provinces, and was known as Gardner's Horse. This corps became the 2nd Bengal Lancers.

In 1823 Regiments of Irregular Horse were redesignated as Local Horse and given serial numbers, and a revised establishment laid down (G.O.C.C., 6th May 1823).

The Local Horse, which, as the G.O.C.C. explains, being neither clothed nor armed by the State, take rank after the infantry, were :

1st (Skinner's) Local Horse.
2nd (Gardner's) Local Horse.
3rd (Blair's) Local Horse.
4th (Baddeley's) Local Horse (became 3rd Skinner's Horse).
5th (Gough's) Local Horse.

The establishment of British officers with Regiments of Local Horse was : a Commandant, Second in Command, Adjutant, and a medical officer.

It is wished here to emphasise the great difference between Local Horse and the Regular Regiments of Bengal Light Cavalry with their large establishment of British officers and N.C.O.s.

In 1840 Regiments of Local Horse were redesignated " Irregular Cavalry " (G.G.O., No. 726), this being consequent on the difficulty the 3rd Skinner's Horse, or the 4th Local Horse, as it then was, experienced in obtaining rations from the commissariat in Afghanistan. In Part III it is recorded how the 4th Local Horse, not being entitled to rations as Local Horse, were allowed to starve during the First Afghan War until the objections of the Audit Department of those days were overcome by this change of designation. For establishment see pages 35, 38, and 95.

In 1857 there were in the Bengal Army ten Regiments of Regular Light Cavalry, and eighteen Regiments of Irregular Cavalry. During the Mutiny all the ten Regiments of Light Cavalry mutinied or were disbanded for disaffection, and, of the eighteen Regiments of Irregular Cavalry only eight survived the reorganisation, which was carried out in 1861 (G.G.O., No. 494) of the confused crowd of Regiments, which the storm of the mutiny had left to represent the Bengal Army.

The eight Regiments which had shown themselves " proof against temptation, fanaticism and threats " (G.G.O. No. 1277 of 9th September 1859) are given below with the new numbers and designation allotted them :

1st Irregular Cavalry became the 1st Bengal Cavalry, and later 1st D.Y.O. Skinner's Horse.
2nd Irregular Cavalry became the 2nd Bengal Cavalry, and later 2nd Gardner's Horse.

4th Irregular Cavalry became the 3rd Bengal Cavalry, and later 3rd Skinner's Horse.

6th Irregular Cavalry became the 4th Bengal Cavalry, and later 4th Cavalry.

7th Irregular Cavalry became the 5th Bengal Cavalry, and later 5th Cavalry.

8th Irregular Cavalry became the 6th Bengal Cavalry, and later 6th K.E.O. Cavalry.

17th Irregular Cavalry became the 7th Bengal Cavalry, and later 7th Hariana Lancers.

18th Irregular Cavalry became the 8th Bengal Cavalry, and later 8th Cavalry.

On the abolition of the Presidency Armies in 1895, there were nineteen Regiments of Bengal Cavalry. The last eleven, viz. 9 to 19, were irregular corps raised by the Punjab Government either when that country was finally taken over after the Sikh Wars, or during the Mutiny, and incorporated in the Bengal Army in 1861.

These new Regiments of Bengal Cavalry differed in their organisation both from the regiments of Regular Bengal Light Cavalry and regiments of Bengal Irregular Cavalry which they replaced. Their establishment of British officers was larger than that of the old Irregular Cavalry, British officers being placed for the first time in command of squadrons, but they had nothing like the large establishment of British officers and N.C.O.s of the old Regular Bengal Light Cavalry. The large British element in the latter was thought to have robbed the Indian officers of all power and influence over their men.

The new organisation was semi-regular, but on the Silladar system, the men providing both their horses, uniform, and equipment. Each Regiment was organised in six troops, and consisted of :

3 Risaldars, on Rs.300, Rs.250, and Rs.200 respectively.
3 Ressaidars, on Rs.150, Rs.135, and Rs.120.
1 Wurdi-Major, on Rs.130.
6 Jemadars, on Rs.80, Rs.70, and Rs.60.
6 Kot Dafadars, on Rs.47.
48 Dafadars on Rs.38.
6 Nishanbadars, on Rs.38.
6 Trumpeters, on Rs.34.
384 Sowars, on Rs.27.
(See also pages 45 and 49.)

In 1859, when Her Majesty Queen Victoria assumed the Government of India, the Indian Forces of the Honourable East India Company were transferred to the Crown. This affected the Indian Army in little more than name and in the conditions of service of the British officer.

In 1885 Regiments were reorganised into four squadrons in place of the old organisation by " troops " or " risalahs," and ten years later, viz. in 1895, squadrons were designated A, B, C, D. The establishment fixed was ten British officers and 625 Indian ranks, at which it stood in 1914, with the exception that the number of British officers, including the medical officer, had been increased to 13.

The issue of Government rifles marked the first change as regards the supply of arms and equipment to the Irregular Cavalry ; hitherto the men had provided everything themselves. As time went on Regiments had gradually to modify the original Silladar system in an attempt to keep pace with modern improvements.

In 1872 the Horse Chunda Fund was started. The men, instead of mounting themselves, paid a fixed sum of money on joining and were provided by the Regiment with horses.

In 1914 the average sum paid by a Sowar on joining was Rs.250 for his horse, Rs.50 for his half-share of a mule, and approximately Rs.150 for his uniform and equipment. The Government provided rifles, signalling equipment, and certain first-line equipment only. When it is remembered that the pay of the Sowar was only Rs.34 per month, plus from five to eight rupees compensation for dearness of rations, and that in addition to mounting themselves, they had to provide their own transport and tentage and build their own quarters, it is not surprising that the Indian Cavalry who set out for France on the outbreak of the Great War were not as well mounted or equipped as regiments of the B.E.F. from England, but it is equally surprising that they were as good as they were. The 3rd Skinner's Horse mobilised with their full war establishment of horses plus ten per cent. reserve, and their animal wastage during the time they were in France was normal.

In 1920 the Silladar System was finally done away with, and Indian Cavalry came on the same footing as other units

of the Regular Army.   The men received a fixed rate of pay
varying from Rs.300 for a Risaldar Major to Rs.18 for a Sowar,
rations both for men and horses were free, and Regiments
had no longer to provide their own transport.   The supply
of remounts was taken over by the Government, and tentage
equipment and clothing were supplied by ordnance, the men
being placed on a fixed clothing allowance.   To bring them
into line with the home establishment, Regiments were reorganised into a Headquarters, Headquarter Wing, and three
Squadrons.

BRITISH OFFICERS

(See extracts from Bengal Army List, Chapter III.)

In its earliest days the British officers of Skinner's Horse
were as irregular as their men ; with the exception of Fraser,
who belonged to the Civil Service, not one of these officers
was in regular Government employ, and with the exception
of James Skinner, who was made a substantive Lieutenant-
Colonel in 1826, none of them held the King's commission.

As time went on it became the custom to second regular
officers of the H.E.I.C., chiefly from Infantry Battalions, to
Regiments of Local Horse for a tour of duty, and it was not
till 1861, on the reorganisation of the Bengal Cavalry after the
Mutiny that British officers were permanently posted to these
Regiments.   Officers messes were started in 1856.

INDIAN OFFICERS

As their titles imply, the Indian officers were Sirdars, or
influential landowners who commanded bodies of men whom
they raised for service in the Army and for whom they were
entirely responsible.

As it was often difficult for a Sirdar to find his quota of
Khudaspah Sowars, i.e. men who could provide their own
horses and equipment, the practice grew up of Indian officers
entertaining " Bargirs," men whom they provided with horses
and equipment, taking in return two-thirds of their pay.   It
was a remunerative business for an Indian officer of means,
but was greatly abused.   James Skinner himself had as many
as three hundred Bargirs and his brother Robert a hundred.

In 1820 this system of " Bargirs " was abolished, but the

order occasioned much dissatisfaction, and was modified two months later, and Indian officers of the first class were allowed to keep not more than three " Bargirs," those of the second class two, and inferior ranks one. A few years later, however, the original system of " Bargirs " was reverted to, but in 1840 a fresh order (G.O.C.C. No. 236) had to be issued restricting the number again.

The following extract of a letter dated Meerut, 21st June 1809, from Colonel Worsley, Adjutant-General of the Army, to Captain Skinner, gives an idea of the disciplinary powers of a C.O. :

" For misconduct Daffadars and Privates may be discharged upon their being pronounced unworthy or unfit by five Native Officers of the Corps, whose opinion in all such cases is to be recorded, and if any Native Officers misbehave in a manner to render themselves unworthy of the service, their conduct is to be reported to the Commander-in-Chief."

DRILL AND EQUIPMENT

In 1835 the English system of drill and English words of command were introduced into Corps of Irregular Horse ; prior to this, Persian words of command had been employed. It was not until the Sikh Wars in the " Forties " that Irregular Corps were brigaded with Regiments of the Line. Generally speaking, each man was armed with a cutting sword, about 15 men per troop carried carbines, and the remainder lances ; but it varied in each Corps, according to the whim of the Officer Commanding. Skinner himself was a great believer in the lance. There is a note in the diary of the 3rd Horse that "jumping" was introduced as part of the drill in 1863.

In 1858 the 1st Skinner's Horse were armed with swords and " percussion carbines of musket bore," which are described by Major Chamberlain as " cumbersome and uncertain weapons, to which he would be sorry to trust his life."

In 1878 snider carbines were issued to replace " the Victoria carbines " which had been in use for ten years.

In 1895 the 3rd Horse obtained permission to arm the front rank with lances (Command Order 407, dated 30th November 1895). The First Corps was converted into a Lancer Regiment in 1896.

DRESS

Strict regard for the dress Regulations has never been a strong point in the Indian Army. In its earliest days Skinner's Horse wore a yellow alkhalak with red turbans and kamarbands, pantaloons coloured with " mooltani matti," in imitation of the leather breeches of the Regulars, and jack-boots. A polished steel " tawah " or helmet, circular at the top, was worn under the turban. A better idea of the uniform can be gathered from the numerous portraits in the Mess.

The 1st Skinner's Horse always retained the famous " yellow " uniform—the red loongi and kamarband being replaced by black ones in 1896. The 3rd Skinner's Horse, on its reorganisation in 1861 as the 3rd Bengal Cavalry, changed to red, and again, from experience gained in the Second Afghan War, to drab. This again in 1890 was changed to blue with yellow facings, and gold lace.

For financial reasons full-dress uniform has not been reinstituted since the Great War, and at the present time Regiments have their field-service khaki only.

APPENDIX B

ROLL OF COMMANDANTS OF THE 1st CORPS OR THE 1st D.Y.O. LANCERS (SKINNER'S HORSE)

Colonel James Skinner, C.B. . .	1803	4.12.41
Major L. H. Smith, 6th L.C. . .	5.12.41	9.11.49
Colonel C. T. Chamberlain . . .	10.11.49	4.8.67
Colonel W. R. E. Alexander . .	5.8.67	31.3.76
Colonel R. Jenkins	1.4.76	9.9.80
Colonel A. R. Chapman . . .	10.9.80	9.9.87
Colonel R. Morris	10.9.87	9.9.94
Lieutenant-Colonel R. F. Gartside Tipping, C.B.	10.9.94	9.9.01
Colonel C. B. Hayes	10.9.01	31.3.07
Colonel C. Davis	1.4.07	31.3.12
Lieutenant-Colonel C. Bailey . .	1.4.12	4.12.14
Lieutenant-Colonel P. Holland Pryor, M.V.O.	5.12.14	6.7.16
Lieutenant-Colonel and Brevet-Colonel F. D. Russell	7.7.16	6.7.20
Lieutenant-Colonel L. E. Dening .	1.12.20	18.5.21

APPENDIX C

ROLL OF COMMANDANTS OF THE 2ND CORPS, OR THE 3RD SKINNER'S HORSE

Local Major Robert Skinner	1814
Major W. C. Baddeley, 24th N.I.	1821
Major C. M. Carmichael Smyth, 3rd L.C. . . .	1824
Major W. Alexander, 5th L.C.	1838
Bt. Lieutenant-Colonel C. E. T. Oldfield, C.B., 5th L.C.	1842
Major R. Cautley, 10th L.C.	1844
Major R. Hill, 70th N.I.	1845
Major A. Martin, 33rd N.I.	1850
Colonel G. W. M. Hall, C.B.	1859
Lieutenant-Colonel G. A. Brownlow	1875
Colonel A. R. D. Mackenzie	1878
Colonel G. W. Willock	1887
Colonel E. A. Money, C.B.	1892
Colonel G. H. Elliott.	1894
Colonel H. J. J. Middleton.	1899
Colonel A. N. Carr	1905
Colonel W. E. A. Blakeney	1908
Colonel E. W. Wall, C.M.G.	1913
Lieutenant-Colonel J. R. Gaussen, C.M.G., C.I.E., D.S.O.	1918
Lieutenant-Colonel E. C. W. Conway-Gordon, C.I.E., p.s.c.	1920

APPENDIX D

LIST OF HONOURS GAINED IN THE FIELD BY BRITISH OFFICERS, INDIAN OFFICERS, AND OTHER RANKS ON THE ACTIVE LIST OF THE 1st DUKE OF YORK'S OWN LANCERS (SKINNER'S HORSE) DURING THE GREAT WAR, INCLUDING THE 3rd AFGHAN WAR 1919.

Colonel Bailey, mentioned in despatches, London Gazette 30.6.16.

Lieutenant-Colonel P. Holland-Pryor, M.V.O., mentioned in despatches, London Gazette 4.7.16, 15.8.17, 12.3.18, 27.8.18, 21.2.19 ; Brevet of Colonel, C.B., C.M.G., D.S.O.

Lieutenant-Colonel F. D. Russell, mentioned in despatches, London Gazette 1.1.16, 3.6.16, and 20.5.20 (Supplement ; Brevets Lieutenant-Colonel and Colonel.

Major J. M. Binny, mentioned in despatches, London Gazette 20.3.16, 12.3.18, and 3.8.20.

Major R. B. C. Raban, mentioned in despatches. Killed in action.

Major A. Chamberlayne, mentioned in despatches. Killed in action.

Major J. A. Muirhead, mentioned in despatches, London Gazette 4.1.16, 15.5.17, and 12.1.20 ; Brevet Lieutenant-Colonel, D.S.O.

Major E. H. Pott, mentioned in despatches, London Gazette 4.1.17, 5.5.17 ; D.S.O.

Captain A. A. H. Beaman, mentioned in despatches, London Gazette 4.7.16; D.S.O. ; French Croix de Guerre.

Captain M. M. Stevenson, mentioned in despatches, London Gazette 3.8.20.

Captain Zorawar Singh, mentioned in despatches, M.C., London Gazette 21.6.16.

Captain A. E. Deane, mentioned in despatches, London Gazette 22.1.19.

Second-Lieutenant Ewart, M.C.

Risaldar Major Mohd Akram Khan, O.B.I., 1st Class, No. 1 of 1920 ; Promoted Hon. Captain.

Hon. Lieutenant Habibur Rahman Khan, Khan Sahib, C.I.E., O.B.I., 2nd Class, No. 3159 of 1919.

Risaldar Ghulam Mohd Khan, 1.7.20, O.B.I., 2nd Class; Promoted Hon. Lieutenant.

Risaldar Faiz Mohd Khan, I.O.M., 2nd Class, No. 819 of 1915,

Risaldar Mardan Khan, Sword of Honour; O.B.I., 2nd Class, No. 1219 of 1917.

Risaldar Nathe Khan, O.B.I., 2nd Class, No. 1629 of 1918.

Jemadar Mohd Taki Khan, D.S.M., Gazette of India, No. 693 of 1920.

Jemadar Rukkan-ud-Din, I.D.S.M., No. 103 of 1916.

Jemadar Mohd Umar Faruq, I.O.M., 2nd Class, No. 1359 of 1917.

No. 1735 Sowar Nishan Ali, I.O.M., 2nd Class, No. 820 of 1915.

Trumpeter Abdul Majid, I.D.S.M., No. 103 of 1916.

JANGI INAM AND LAND

Risaldar Major and Hon. Captain Mohd Akram Khan, 2 squares of land.

Risaldar and Hon. Lieutenant Ghulam Mohd Khan, 2 squares of land.

Risaldar Ghulam Kadar Khan, Jangi Inam.

Jemadar Mahfuz Ali Khan, 2 squares of land.

Jemadar Umar Faruq, Jangi Inam.

Dafadar Molaim Khan, 1 square of land.

Dafadar Ghulam Mohd, 1 square of land.

Dafadar Ali Hassan, 1 square of land.

Dafadar Mohd Mahmud Ali Khan, Jangi Inam.

Dafadar Talemand Khan, Jangi Inam.

Dafadar Mohd Ishak Khan, Jangi Inam.

Dafadar Ashrafullah Khan, Jangi Inam.

Lance-Dafadar Imam Ali Khan, Jangi Inam.

Lance-Dafadar Nur Mohd Khan, Jangi Inam.

Sowar Mohd Amir Khan, Jangi Inam.

Sowar Abdul Razzak, Jangi Inam.

Sowar Ali Zaman Khan, Jangi Inam.

Sowar Mazhar Ali Khan, Jangi Inam.

Sowar Mohd Yusaf Khan, Jangi Inam.

Sowar Ashak Ali Khan, Jangi Inam.

Maulvi Hafiz Ahmed Beg, Jangi Inam.

Syce Nabi Bakhsh, Jangi Inam.

LIST OF HONOURS GAINED IN THE FIELD BY BRITISH OFFICERS, INDIAN OFFICERS, AND OTHER RANKS ON THE ACTIVE SERVICE LIST OF THE 3RD SKINNER'S HORSE DURING THE GREAT WAR, INCLUDING THE 3RD AFGHAN WAR 1919, AND OPERATIONS WAZIRISTAN FORCE.

Colonel E. W. Wall, mentioned in despatches, London Gazette 15.6.16, 1.6.17, and 3.2.20 ; promoted Colonel, C.M.G.

Lieutenant-Colonel J. R. Gaussen, D.S.O., mentioned in despatches, London Gazette 15.6.16 and 1.5.20; C.M.G., C.I.E.

Lieutenant-Colonel E. C. W. Conway-Gordon, mentioned in despatches, London Gazette 1.6.16, 11.12.17, and 3.8.20 ; C.I.E.

Major C. B. Stokes, mentioned in despatches four times. Brevet Lieutenant-Colonel; C.I.E., D.S.O., O.B.E.

Major M. R. H. Webber, mentioned in despatches, London Gazette 13.5.24; O.B.E.

Major V. A. Coaker, mentioned in despatches, London Gazette 1.6.17 and 3.8.20 ; D.S.O.

Major H. E. Medlicott, mentioned in despatches, London Gazette 15.6.16, 11.12.17, 20.5.18, and 3.8.20 ; Brevet Major, D.S.O., Belgian War Cross, French War Cross.

Major T. E. Hulbert, mentioned in despatches, London Gazette 11.6.20 ; O.B.E.

Major R. W. Manderson, mentioned in despatches, London Gazette 12.3.18, 27.8.18, 12.2.19 ; O.B.E.

Major A. M. Daniels, mentioned in despatches, London Gazette 15.5.17, 15.8.17, 27.8.18, 5.6.19, and 13.3.25 ; Brevet Major, O.B.E.

Major J. M. Lorimer, mentioned in despatches.

Major E. D. Metcalfe, mentioned in despatches, London Gazette 15.8.17 ; M.C.

Captain H. H. Lyons, M.C., mentioned in despatches ; awarded Bar to M.C. in 1919.

Captain A. R. Jefferis, mentioned in despatches, M.B.E.

Risaldar Major Balwant Singh, O.B.I., 2nd Class, subsequently promoted 1st Class, No. 959 of 1916.

Risaldar Major Nur Mohd Khan, mentioned in despatches
15.6.16; awarded O.B.I., 2nd Class.

Jemadar Amin Lall, awarded M.C., Gazette of India, No. 89,
dated 11.1.19.

Jemadar Indar Singh, awarded I.O.M., 2nd Class, Gazette of
India, No. 934 of 1919.

Jemadar Delel Singh, mentioned in despatches, Gazette of
India, No. 348, dated 2.2.19.

Jemadar Bhagwan Singh, mentioned in despatches, Gazette
of India, No. 1846, dated 10.9.20.

1310 Dafadar Zahur Ali Khan, Croix de Guerre (French),
No. 361 of 1916.

602 Dafadar Kutab Khan, Bronze Medal for Military Valour
(Italian), No. 1869 of 1919.

883 Dafadar Nand Singh, I.O.M.S., No. 1365 of 1920.

1307 Dafadar Chajja Singh, awarded M.S.M. without annuity,
Gazette of India, No. 755, dated 23.4.20.

1389 Dafadar Jawahar Singh, awarded I.O.M., 2nd Class,
Gazette of India, No. 3155, dated 24.10.19.

1559 Lance-Dafadar Ramchandar, mentioned in despatches,
Gazette of India, No. 348, dated 24.10.19.

1267 Lance-Dafadar Nahar Singh, I.M.S. Medal, No. 2361 of
1920.

Dafadar Lall Singh, awarded I.O.M. in 1918, 881 of 1919.

Lance-Dafadar Kjem Singh, awarded I.O.M. in 1918, 881 of 1919.

1450 Dafadar Gurdial Singh, mentioned in despatches, Gazette
of India, No. 1846, dated 10.9.20, awarded I.D.S.M. 1919,
No. 2 of 1920.

1691 A. L. D. Pretam Singh, mentioned in despatches, Gazette
of India, No. 1846, dated 10.9.20.

1012 Sowar Pokhar Singh, mentioned in despatches, Gazette
of India, No. 348, dated 24.10.19.

1546 Sowar Chajja Singh, mentioned in despatches, Gazette
of India, No. 1845, dated 10.9.20.

Jangi Inam and Land

Risaldar Major Balwant Singh, land.
Jemadar Amin Lall, land.
Dafadar Lall Singh, land.
Risaldar Amar Singh, Jangi Inam.

Risaldar Major Wali Dada Khan, land.
Risaldar Bhagwan Singh, land.*
Risaldar Nur Mohd Khan, Jangi Inam.
Risaldar Major Sheo Chand, land.
Dafadar Quaah Khan, land.
Dafadar Chajja Singh, land.
Sowar Adbul Razzak Khan, land.
Jemadar Indar Singh, Jangi Inam.
Jemadar Asghar Ali Khan, Jangi Inam.
Dafadar Nizan ud Din, Jangi Inam.
Dafadar Kallu Singh, Jangi Inam.
Jemadar Zahur Ali Khan, Jangi Inam.
Dafadar Jawahar Singh, Jangi Inam.
Risaldar Chanwad Singh, Jangi Inam.
Risaldar Major Sheo Chand, Jangi Inam.
Jemadar Gopal Dass, Jangi Inam.
Dafadar Kehar Singh, Jangi Inam.
Ressaidar Mohan Singh, land.
Ressaidar Udai Singh, Jangi Inam.
Sowar Kesho Singh,* land given to Risaldar Bhagwan Singh.
Jemadar Syed Abdul Majid, Jangi Inam.
Ressaidar Harnarain Singh, Jangi Inam.
Dafadar Sarwan Singh, Jangi Inam.
K. Dafadar Chandan Singh, Jangi Inam.
L. D. Ganeshi Singh, Jangi Inam.
A. L. D. Arjan Singh, Jangi Inam.
Dafadar Chandar Singh, Jangi Inam.
Dafadar Nahar Singh, Jangi Inam.
S. A. S. Syed Ahmed, Jangi Inam.
K. Dafadar Kehar Singh, Jangi Inam.
A. L. D. Mohd Shafi, Jangi Inam.
Dafadar Shadal Khan, Jangi Inam.
Munshi Bachu Singh, Jangi Inam vice Risaldar Bhagwan Khan.

*Printed in Great Britain by Hazell, Watson & Viney, Ld.,
London and Aylesbury.*

1316133R0

Printed in Germany
by Amazon Distribution
GmbH, Leipzig